MUGHAL ADMINISTRATION

SIR JADUNATH SARKAR

SANAGE
PUBLISHING HOUSE

Paperback: 978-936205531-6
Hardback: 978-936205300-8
eBook: 978-936205345-9

Printed by:

Sanage Publishing House LLP
Mumbai, India

sanagepublishing@gmail.com

Sir Jadunath Sarkar, CIE, FRAS (10 December 1870 – 19 May 1958) was a prominent Indian historian and a specialist on the Mughal dynasty. Sarkar was educated in English literature, worked as a teacher for some period of time but later shifted his focus to history research writing. He had vast knowledge of Persian language and all his books he wrote in English.

Contents

CHAPTER I.

THE GOVERNMENT: ITS CHARACTER & AIMS

§1. The aspects of Mughal administration studied in this book.

We are all familiar with the history of the Mughal empire in India, —the long story of the successive Emperors, their wars for the throne of Delhi, their campaigns against their rebellious vassals and independent neighbours, and their expeditions beyond the natural frontiers of India. We know much about the private lives of the emperors, the ceremony and splendour of their Courts, and the condition of the roads, from the writings of the many European visitors to our land. But their administrative system has not yet been subjected to a detailed study on the basis of the original Persian records.

This is a task of admitted difficulty, partly because so many of the records have perished in the course of time, but mainly because it is only men experienced in the actual conduct of modern Indian administration who can go to the very heart of the Mughal system and make the dead past live again before our eyes. The great historian of the Decline and Fall of the Roman Empire has confessed that his experience as a captain in the English militia* and as a member of the British Parliament enabled him to understeind aright the campaigns of the Roman generals and the debates of the ancient Romain Senate. We who are closet students of Indian history can deal only with old paper, with MS. records of the past; we can touch only the exterior of the Mughal system. But the real working of that system, its inner springs and practical effect can be best understood only by men who combine a knowledge of Persiein historical manuscripts with experience in the administration of the people of the provinces once subject to Mughal rule,—i.e., by scholarly members of the Indian Civil Service in Upper India, Among them have been Mr.

Edward Thomas, the distinguished father of an equally distinguished son, Mr. H. Beveridge, who was once Judge in this very town (Patna), Mr. William Irvine, who was long magistrate of Ghzizipur and Saharanpur, Mr. John Beaimes and some other civil officers, whose studies in certain aispects of the Mughal administration,—especially the revenue system, —are extremely fruitful and corrective of the errors of popular writers.

* "The discipline and evolution of a modern battalion gave me a clearer notion of the phalanx and the legion, and the captain of the Hampshire grenadiers has not been useless to the historian of the Roman Empire." (Gibbon's Memoirs.)

Now, modern European writers have studied only two departments of the Mughal administration in detail, namely the land revenue and the army. Practically full information on these two subjects is available in English. I shall, therefore, leave them out of my course of lectures except in respect of some minor points where I can supply additional information from manuscripts unknown to my predecessors.

The first of the following lectures will deal with the principles and distinctive characteristics of the Mughal government ; the second with the Emperor's power, the position of his ministers, the departments of the State, the functions of the chief officers, and our sources of information; the third will make a minute study of the diwan and the procedure of his office and the work of the Lord High Steward and his assistant; the fourth will discuss the piovincial administration; the fifth will concern itself with the State in relation to the ryot; and the concluding lecture will attempt a philosophical survey of the influence of Mughal rule on the country and the causes of the decline of the Mughal Empire.

§2. Traces of Mughal rule in our living present.

The administrative system of the Mughal empire has more than an academic interest for us. This type of administration, with its arrangement's procedure machinery and even titles, was borrowed by the Hindu States outside the territory directly subject to Muslim rule. It would not be a surprise to see the Mughal system copied by the vassal Rajahs of Jaipur or Bundelkhand, just as in our own day the British system is faithfully copied by the darbars of Baroda and Gwalior, Indore and Alwar. But the Mughal system was also the model followed by some independent Hindu States of the time. Even a staunch champion of Hindu orthodoxy like Shivaji at first copied it in Maharashtra and it was only later in life that he made a deliberate attempt to give a Hindu colour to his administrative machinery by substituting Sanskrit titles for Persian ones at his Court but most of the names of departments, records and subordinate officials in his kingdom remained Islamic, where they were not indigenous Marathi.

Thus, the Mughal system at one time spread over practically all the civilised and organised parts of India.

Nor is it altogether dead in our own times. Traces of it still survive and an observant student of history can detect the Mughal substructure under the modern British Indian administrative edifice. When in the late 18th century a band of English merchants and clerks were unexpectedly called upon to govern a strange land and an alien race, they very naturally took over the Mughal system then prevailing among the people, made in it only the most necessary changes and while retaining its old frame-work, they very reluctantly and slowly added such new elements as the safety and prosperity of the country demanded from time to time. This was the true character of the Anglo- Indian administration of Bengal and Bihar under Warren Hastings. Under his successors, after many intervals of repose, the administration has again and again departed from its Mughal original. But the new has been built upon the old; our present has its roots in our past.

§3. The aims of the Mughal State.

Before we can understand the Mughal administrative system correctly, it is necessary for us to realise its nature and aims.

By its nature it was a military rule and therefore necessarily a centralised despotism. To the Mus im portion of the population the sovereign was the head of both Church and State and therefore for them he undertook socialistic functions. But towards his non-Muslun subjects he followed the policy of the individualistic minimum of interference, i.e., he was content with discharging only the police duties and the collection of revenue. The support of public education was not a duty of the State, — indeed, it was recognised as a national duty even in England as late as 1870. According to Hindu and Muhammadan political thought alike, education was the handmaid of religion. If the king spent anything on education, it was not an act of State but a private religious benefaction for acquiring personal merit in the next world. Some schools were subsidised by the Padishahs, but it was only because they were attached to mosques or taught by families of holy men already in receipt of imperial bounty or in other words because they served as seminaries for training ulema (theologians) for the service of the State Church.

Similarly, the encouragement of art and literature was a purely personal matter with the king; its aim was to procure him personal recreation or glorification, and not to promote national culture. Here the head of the State was exactly on the same footing as a rich private citizen, and he recognised no higher obligation to his people.

In short, under Mughal rule the socialistic activities—I use the word in its broadest sense, —of a modern State were left to the community, to society, or the caste brotherhood and the student of Indian administration has to pass over them in silence.

The aim of the government was thus extremely limited, materialistic, almost sordid.

A minute study of the history of the Mughal empire in India on the basis of State papers and other original sources, impresses us with certain facts as broadly characteristic of the administration.

§4. The imported foreign elements in the Mughal administrative system.

First, the Mughal governmental system took its colour from the race and creed of its sovereigns. They were a foreign Muhammadan dynasty who settled in India eight centuries after Islam had been adopted in certain countries outside India and a new administrative type had been developed in those countries.

Our Turkish conquerors brought with themselves to their new home the type of administration which had long been known to extra-Indian Muslim countries as the model and which had been proved by the experience of centuries as the most successful, viz., the administrative system of the Abbasid Khalifs of Iraq and the Fatimid Khalifs of Egypt. The Mughal administration presented a combination of Indian and extra-

Indian elements or more correctly, it was the Perso-Arabic system in Indian setting.

The principles of their government, their church policy, their rules of taxation, their departmental arrangements and the very titles of their officials were imported ready-made from outside India. But a compromise was affected with the older native system already in possession of the field and familiar to the people governed. The details of the imported system were modified to suit local needs. The existing Indian practice and the vast mass of Indian customary law were respected so far as they did not run counter to the root principles of all Islamic governments; and in all non-essential matters, in the spectacular side of politics,* and generally speaking, in village administration and the lower rungs of the official ladder, the Indian usage was allowed to prevail, while the foreign model swayed almost exclusively the Court (which was a personal matter for the sovereign) and the higher official circles, (who drew their inspiration from Persia and Egypt.)

This foreign element in the Mughal administration can be easily illustrated from the provincial administration. As Professor C. H. Becker of Hamburg writes in the Encyclopaedia of Islam: "In the early centuries of Arab rule two political functions were sharply distinguished [in Egypt, viz.,] the governorship and the treasury. The governor, [called] amir, had control over the military and police only... Alongside of him was the head of the treasury, [called] the amil... These two officers had to keep a strict watch on one another. As head of the military and executive, the amir was the first [in authority] but they were equal in rank and the administrator of the treasury even had the greater influence [over the sovereign.]" (Encyclopeadia of Islam, Vol II. P. 13.)

---

* Lord Clive performed the punyah ceremony at Murshidabad! Here we have a Hindu revenue usage coming down from very ancient times through the Muhammadan age to the early British period.

Now, this was exactly the relation between the subahdar or provincial governor and the diwan or revenue chief of the province. A concrete illustration of the official antagonism between the two and their mutual recriminations to their master—for, it was the duty of each, in the words of Prof. Becker, "to keep a strict watch over the other, —can be found in my account of the history of Orissa in the 17th century, based on contemporary official papers, published in the Journal of the Bihar and Orissa Research Society in June and Sept., 1916 and reprinted in my Studies in Mughal India, pp. 221—224.

So, too, in the division of the administration into departments the model of Islamic lands outside India was followed.

The second characteristic is that the Government was military in its origin and though in time it became rooted to the soil it retained its military character to the last. Every offcial of the Mughal Government had to be enrolled in the army list; he was given a mansab as the nominal commander of so many horsemen, which determined his pay and status. Civil servants, judges of Canon Law, superintendents of post excise or customs and even clerks and accountants of the higher grades were all ranked as mansabdars, i.e., members of the army. Their names were arranged in the gradation-list of the army, they were paid by the Bakhshis or military paymasters and their promotion took the form of an increase in their nominal command. From this it followed that the Treasury or spending department of the Government was only one for the civil and military services alike or in strict theory there was no civil Treasury at all. We should, however, remember that though the salary-bills were passed by the Bakhshis or military paymasters, the actual payment (except to the field army during a campaign) was made by the Diwan, who was reckoned as a civil officer.

Thirdly, the main point to be noted about the land revenue system of Mughal India is its long and close adherence to the old practice, procedure and even tradition of the country. Indeed, the early Muhammadan conquerors very wisely retained the old Hindu revenue system intact, employed the old Hindu revenue officials and seldom interfered with the working of this department so long as the land-tax was regularly collected and there was no striking default or peculation.

This remark is true of the land revenue alone, which has always been the most traditional and conservative branch of Government activity in India. But in the case of the other sources of State income, the Quranic law and the practice of older Islamic States outside India exercised their full influence and we find in Indo-Muhammadan history repeated attempts to adjust the actual practice of the Government in the revenue department to the theory of the Canon Law of Islam in this matter.* Thus, the entire revenue system of the Mughal empire as it was developed in the 17th century was a resultant of two forces,—the time-honoured Hindu practice and the abstract Arabian theory.

Between these two discordant elements the compromise was not always happy or successful, and the dead weight of Indian usage in the end proved too heavy for the orthodox zeal of Quranic pursuits like Firuz Shah Tughlaq or Aurangzib. When they closed their eyes or even in their lifetime, after a brief span of strict adherence to the Quranic precept and abolition of "innovations" (bida't), things fell back into their old traditional grooves. The subject will be more fully discussed in a subsequent lecture.

---

* *E g., Firuz Shah Tughlaq (in Elliot, iii. 377.)*

§5. The State as a manufacturer.

Fourthly, in Mughal India the State was the largest manufacturer, or rather the only manufacturer on a large-scale in respect of several commodities. The modern practice of Government buying ready-made goods in the open market or giving orders for large quantities to contractors, would not have answered in those days of cottage industries, when production on a large scale with a view to sale by private capitalists was unknown. The State was, therefore, forced to manufacture the commodities it needed.

And its need was very large. Twice every year, —in the rainy season and the winter, — a robe (khelat) suitable for the season was presented by the emperor to every mansabdar and the number of mansabdars in 1690 is given as nearly 7,500 who were paid in cash and 4,000 who held jagirs. (Z. 15 a.) For the higher nobles, one suit of the robe of honour consisted of several articles of apparel. In addition to these two seasonal gifts, the princes of the blood, the vassal Rajahs and many of the mansabdars and Court officials received robes of honour at the two birthdays of the Emperor (viz. according to the lunar and the solar calculations), the lunar anniversary of his coronation, the two I'ds and down to Aurangzib's reign on the old Persian New Year's Day, when the Sun enters the Aries (nau-roz). As a matter of rule khelats were also bestowed on most persons when they were presented at Court or took leave or were appointed to posts and for some time in Aurangzib's reign, on converts to Islam.

It will thus be seen that the Imperial Government had to keep a vast stock of cloth and ready-made robes for its need during the year. The supply was assured by the State maintaining many factories (karkhanahs) of its own in the principal cities of the empire, where skilled workmen were brought together (sometimes from distant provinces), placed under a Government superintendent (darogha), paid daily wages and made to produce their handicrafts which were duly stocked in the stores.

The same thing was done with regard to various articles of consumption cind luxury required by the emperor's household. It was the business of the Khan-i-saman or Lord High Steward to buy such goods as were available in the market and manufacture the others well in advance of the time when they would be required. A detailed study of the karkhanahs will give us an idea of the immense field of State activity in the industrial sphere.

Fifthly, the Mughal Government was a highly centralised autocracy. The Crown was the motive power of the entire administrative machinery. Where the Government is absolute, the supreme authority concentrated in one man's hand, the territory large, the means of communication between the districts slow and difficult, the transfer of local officers frequent and no political life or local initiative left to the people, —there the natural consequence is the multiplication of official correspondence and the growth of a vast mass of written records. The Mughal Government, except in the actual conducting of campaigns, was a kaghazi raj, i.e., paper Government. Its officers had to maintain many books, such as copies of correspondence, nominal rolls, descriptive rolls, history of the services of officers, newsletters and despatches received, as well as accounts in duplicate or triplicate, summary or full, —besides keeping an army of spies and couriers for the information of the central Government.

§6. Law and justice.

Sixthly, its attitude towards law and justice was opposed to our conceptions. One of the most essential functions of a modern State is the administration of justice and the maintenance of order. Herein the Mughal Government was weakest and least capable of improvement and expansion with time. It, no doubt, undertook to defend the country from foreign invasion and internal revolt, and to protect life and property in the cities by its own agents. But the policing of the vast rural areas was left to the locality; it was done by the local chaukidars who were servants of the village community and maintained by the villagers themselves out of the villageland and who were not considered as officers paid and supervised by the State. Instead of the Mughal Government undertaking responsibility for rural peace and security, it made the villagers responsible for the safety of their own property and that of travellers in the neighbouring roads. There was, no doubt, a government agent there, viz., the faujdar but his jurisdiction was too large to allow him to attempt the supervision of the police of all the villages in that region. His recognised duty was to prevent or punish wide-spread or notorious acts of violence, such as rebellion by local zamindars, organised raids by large gangs of robbers or the withholding of land revenue on a large scale.

As regards justice, the Mughal Emperor loved to pose as the fountain of justice and followed the immemorial Eastern tradition that the king should try cases himself in open court. Both Shah Jahan and Aurangzib held no public darbar on Wednesday but reserved that day for holding a court of law. "The Emperor came direct from the darshan window to the diwand-i-khas (or Hall of Private Audience) at about 8 A.M. and sat on the throne of justice till midday. This room was filled with the law-officers of the Crown, the judges of Canon Law (qazis), judges of Common Law (adils), muftis, theologians (ulema), jurists learned in precedents (fatawa), the superintendent of the law-court, (darogha-i-adalat) and the kotwal or prefect of the city police. No one else among the courtiers was admitted unless his presence was especially necessary. The officers of justice presented the plaintiffs one by one and reported their grievances. His Majesty very gently ascertained the facts by inquiry, took the law from the ulema and pronounced judgment accordingly. Many persons had come from far-off provinces to get justice from the highest power in the land. Their plaints could not be investigated except locally and so the Emperor wrote orders to the governors of those places, urging them to find out the truth and either do them justice there or send the parties back to the capital with their reports." (Studies in Mughal India, pp. 14 and 70.)

The Emperor was the highest court of appeal and sometimes acted as the court of first instance, too. But, from the nature of things, only a few plaintiffs could reach his throne and he could spare time for adjudicating only a small portion of the appeals that were handed to him, though several of the Mughal Emperors, notably Jahangir, made a parade of their devotion to duty by hanging a golden chain from their palace-balcony to the ground outside Agra fort, to which the people in the streets could tie their petitions for royal justice in order to be drawn up to the Emperor, without their having to grease the palms of the palace porters and underlings, courtiers and other middlemen.

The main defect of the department of law and justice was that there was no system, no organisation of the law-courts in a regular gradation from the highest to the lowest, nor any proper distribution of courts in proportion to the area to be served by them.

Every provincial capital had its qazi, appointed by the Supreme Qazi of the Empire (the Qazi-ul-quzat); but there were no lower or primary courts under him and therefore no provincial court of appeal. The smaller towns and all the villages which had no qazi of their own, seem to have formed a sort of no-man's land as regards justice, though any plaintiff living in them, if he was sufficiently rich and enterprising, could carry his suit to the qazi of the province.

As the provincial qazi's jurisdiction was very vast and he had no assistant or deputy legally competent to share his burden, only a small part of the disputes in the provinces could be tried by him. The Indian villager in the Mughal Empire was denied the greatest pleasure of his life in our own times, viz., facility for civil litigation with Government courts of first instance close at his doors and an abundance of courts of appeal rising up to the High Court at the capital.

Men had, therefore, to settle their differences locally, by appeal to the caste courts or panchayets, the arbitration of an impartial umpire (salis), or by a resort to force.

The crudeness and insufficiency of the judicial system was aggravated by the fact that the only law recognised by the Emperor and his judges was the Quranic law, which had originated and grown to maturity outside India. It was supposed to have been defined once for all within the pages of the Quran as revealed to the Arabian Prophet. But there was a wide latitude in the interpretation of the words of the Quran. And for this purpose, our Indian judges turned to the known decisions of the pious Muslim kings and eminent Muslim jurists of the past, in the chief centres of Islamic thought and civilisation outside India. Thus, Muslim law in India did not originate in legislation but in revelation; it had two other sources, viz., precedents or case-laws and the opinions of jurists, though both of these latter merely professed to make the meaning of the Quran explicit and not to add any new principle or rule to what is written in the Book of God.

All the three sources of Indo-Muhammadan law were trans-Indian. No Indian Emperor or Qazi's decision was ever considered authoritative enough to lay down a legal principle, elucidate any obscurity in the Quran, or supplement the Quranic law by following the line of its obvious intention in respect of cases not explicitly provided for by it.

Hence, it became necessary for Indian Qazis to have at their elbow a digest of Islamic law and precedent compiled from the accepted Arabic writers. Such digests were prepared from time to time, and their character varied with the sovereign's choice among the four schools of Islamic law, viz., the Hanafi, the Malaki, the Shafii, and the Hanbali. The Hanafi school was considered orthodox in India. The last law digest prepared in our country was the Fatawa-i-Alamgiri, which was compiled by a syndicate of theologians under orders of Aurangzib at a cost of two lakhs of Rupees. Muslim Law in India was, therefore, incapable of growth and change, except so far as it reflected changes of juristic thought in Arabia or Egypt.

As is well-known to students of mediæval history, in a Muslim State the Civil Law is merged in and subordinated to the Canon Law, and the theologicins are the only jurists.

We have no information about the Hindu, caste courts and arbitration boards which administered justice according to Common Law, nor about the Brahmanic courts sanctioned by the emperor Akbar, which followed Manu and other text-writers on the "Gentoo Code," as Nathaniel B. Halhed called the loose mass of Hindu legal rules and pious injunctions which were appealed to by Hindu litigants at the end of the Mughal period.

§7. The State declines all socialistic functions.

Of the provincial administration little need, be said. The work at the headquarters of the province, viz. that of the local subahdar, diwan and qazi, followed the well-known lines of their counterpart at the imperial Court. As has been well remarked by a Emropean writer, "Every subahdar tried to play the Padishah in his own province."

But of the political and economic life of the people, especially in the villages, no account has survived and for a sufficient reason. The State in those days, as I have already pointed out, contented itself with the police duties and revenue collection, * and did not undertake any socialistic work, nor interfere with the lives of the villagers, so long as there was no violent crime or defiance of royal authority in the locality. Every village was left free to continue the noiseless even tenor of its life along the old grooves, untroubled by Government, if it did not trouble the Government. The State refused to take the initiative in social progress, or the economic development of the people (as distinct from the domains of the crown or khalsa sharifa, where it was like a private landlord) or the promotion of literature or art (except for the emperor's personal gratification) or the improvement of communication (except for military purposes.) All these things, where done at all, were done by private enterprise. Where there was any organised village community the initiative in these matters was taken by the headman or council of village elders, in all other places, the centre of local life was the zamindar or petty rajah.

The policy of benevolent interference and paternal guidance of the lives of the people adopted by the Buddhist Emperor Asoka in his empire 250 years before the birth of Christ, was not attempted by the Mughal Emperors after Akbar's reign. Wherever the Mughal local officers showed too active an interest in local life (outside the provincial capital), it was against superior orders and in consequence of a corrupt love of gain or spirit of partisanship. And the result of such interference was always bad.

* "Administrative nihilism," as Huxley called it, or "anarchy plus the policeman."

Large empires of a mediaeval stationary type of civilisation and inhabited by diverse tribes, like the Chinese Empire, have held together, only because the central Government has wisely let the rural areas alone, giving to the people of each district freedom to live their lives according to immemorial usage if they supplied the fixed quota of local troops and their fixed share of the revenue of the State.

There was, therefore, something like local autonomy. But the geographical units enjoying such autonomy were so small and their activities were so purely municipal and social, that it would be more correct to say that the villages and small towns of the Mughal Empire enjoyed parochial self-government rather than local autonomy. In the absence of political freedom and power of self-taxation for communal (as distinct from sectarian or caste) purposes, there cannot be any local autonomy.

CHAPTER II.

THE SOVEREIGN AND DEPARTMENTAL HEADS SOURSES.

§1. The Mughal Sovereign's legal position and powers.

According to the theory of the Quranic law, the sovereign is only the commander of the true believers (amir-ul-mumnin) and is responsible to the general body (jamat) of the Muslims for the proper discharge of his duties. But no constitutional machinery for controlling or judging him, such as a parliament or council of ministers responsible to the people, was in existence in any Muhammadan country or even conceived of The Muslim State was essentially a military State and depended for its existence on the absolute authority of the monarch, who was also the supreme general. The Roman Imperator's functions were similar but according to the constitution of Rome, the sanction of the Senate to important measures of State and the popular election of the chief officials were devised as checks (however futile in practice) on the emperor's absolutism. No such check existed in the Islamic world even in theory, though in practice the sovereign's action was often influenced by his fear of the Muslim soldiery and his reluctance to incur social odium.

No doubt, it was open to a number of theologians (ulema) to issue a decree deposing the sovereign as a violator of the Quranic law and therefore unfit to reign. But the only means of enforcing such a decree was a rebellion. There was no constitutional body that could peacefully depose one king and set up another. In fact, the successful removal of a tyrannical Sultan always implied the rise of a pretender with a superior military force at his back. The regular forces of the State were bound to obey the king de facto and not the ulema nor the council of ministers.

The Mughal Emperor had no regular council of ministers. The wazir or diwan was the highest person below the emperor but the other officers were in no sense his colleagues. They were admittedly inferior to him and deserved rather to be called secretaries than ministers because nearly all their work was liable to revision by the wazir, and royal orders were often transmitted to them through him.

As a matter of practice, when the emperor held his private consultation or diwan-i-khas, the other high officers (viz., the chief Paymaster, the chief Qazi, the High Steward, and the Commander-in-chief, if any) usually attended along with the wazir and were consulted. But many important questions were decided by the emperor and the wazir alone without the knowledge of the other ministers. It need hardly be said that neither the lower ministers nor even the wazir could serve as a check on the royal will. They could advise but never vote and the insecurity and dependence of their position made it impossible for them to contradict the king even when he was clearly going wrong. The Mughal government was, therefore, a one-man rule, and Aurangzib, like his contemporary Louis XIV., was really his own prime minister.

From this it will be seen that the Mughal Emperor had no Cabinet in the modern sense of the term. His ministers were mere secretaries who carried out the royal will in matters of detail, but they could never influence his policy except by the arts of gentle persuasion and veiled warning; they never resigned if he rejected their counsels. In short, the ministers directed the administration only when the emperor slept. Such ministerial control was really a violation of the spirit of the constitution (if I may use the name, where the thing did not exist); it indicated a state of anarchy like the periods when the Witenagemot effectively controlled the royal government of Anglo-Saxon England.

The immensity of the Mughal Emperor's power can be judged from the fact that he was the head of the Church and the State alike. Every Muslim sovereign is, in strict theory, the Khalif of the age or the latest successor of the Prophet in the command of the faithful and so long as he is not deposed by the verdict of the Quranic lawyers, his power is supreme.

The Mughal Emperors, like all other Islamic sovereigns, had to play a twofold part, viz., to govern all the people in their dominions as their king and also to be the missionary defender and agent of the creed of a section of their subjects. Therefore, from the Muhammadan portion of their subjects they levied the zakat or tithes, amounting to one-fortieth of every man's annual increase, which they were bound to spend for the benefit of the faithful only, —by building mosques, subsidising pious men and theological teachers, endowing saints' tombs, and monasteries, relieving Muslim paupers and providing dowries for Muslim maidens. This zakat passed into the public treasury in the same way as the land-tax or the custom duty. The best illustration of the emperor's headship of the Church and the State alike is furnished by the fact that in later ages the Muhammadan rulers abused their trust by spending the zakat on their personal needs or for the general purposes of the Government.

§2. The chief departments and their heads.

So much for the sovereign's power, the position of his ministers and the aims of the Government. We shall now study the administrative system in detail.

The chief departments of the Mughal Government were:

The Exchequer and Revenue (under the High Diwan)

2. The Imperial Household (under the Khan-i-saman or High Steward.)

3. The military Pay and Accounts Office (under the imperial Bakhshi.)

4. Canon Law, both civil and criminal, (under the Chief Qazi.)

5. Religious endowments and charity (under the chief Sadr.)

6. Censorship of Public Morals (under the Muhtasib.) Inferior to these but ranking almost like departments, were: —

7. The Artillery (under the Mir Atish or Darogha-i-Topkhanah.) and

8. Intelligence and Posts (under the Darogha of Dak Chauki.)

The innumerable karkhanahs (i.e., factories and stores), each under a darogha or superintendent, were not departments. Most of them were under the Khan-i-saman.

§3. The Wazir or Chancellor.

'Wazir' or prime minister seems to have been an honorific title, without necessarily implying the charge of any particular branch of the administration. He was, no doubt, always the of the revenue department, but it was in his capacity of diwan. All diwans, however, were not wazirs and we read of no Hindu diwan being given the high title of wazir.

Originally the wazir was the highest officer the revenue department, and in the natural course of events control over the other departments gradually passed into his hands. It was only when the king was incompetent, a pleasure-seeker or a minor, that the wazir also controlled the army. Thus, in its origin the wazir's post was a civil one and his assumption of the supreme military direction was abnormal and a mark of imperial decadence. No doubt, the wazir, like every other high official of the Mughal Government was expected to command an army and often did actually lead a short expedition but the necessity of his constant attendance on the Emperor prevented him from taking charge of military operations for a long time or at a distance from the imperial camp.

The wazir 's office received all revenue papers and returns and despatches from the provinces and the field armies. He also acted as the king's representative or many ceremonial occasions. He wrote letters "by order" (hasb-ul-hukm) in his own person though under the emperor's directions. All orders for payment (except for small sums or money previously allotted) had to be signed by the diwan and the payment (except to the field army and the workmen of the State factories) was made through his department only. So, too, all questions connected with the collection of the revenue were decided by the diwan, who consulted the emperor in important cases and frequently reported to him the state of the Treasury. Some of the famous wazirs of the Mughal period were also masters of Persian prose and they acted as secretaries in drafting royal letters to foreign rulers on behalf of their masters.

It was only under the degenerate descendants of Aurangzib that the wazirs became virtual rulers of the State, like the Mayors of the Palace in mediæval France.

§4. The Bakhshi or Paymaster.

Every officer of the Mughal Government was enrolled as a commander of so many horsemen. This title was only a convenient means of calculating his salary and status. It did not mean that he had actually to maintain so many horsemen in his service. Thus, theoretically even the civil officers belonged to the military department and therefore the salary bills of all officers had to be calculated and passed by the paymasters of the army. These paymasters (bakhshis) were increased in number with the growth of the empire, till at the end of Aurangzib's reign we have one chief Bakhshi, called the Mir Bakhshi or Imperial Paymaster popularly as the First Bakhshi, with three assistants called the 2nd, 3rd, and 4th Bakhshis.

Each field army of the Mughal empire was placed under a general appointed for the occasion, being usually a prince of the blood (when available) under the guardianship of a senior noble. Though on several occasions we have officers invested with the title of sipah-salar or 'commander of troops," it was only a mark of honour, and they did not really command the entire Mughal army. The emperor was the only commander-in-chief.

The artillery branch was, however, placed in charge of an officer called the Mir Atish or popularly, Darogha-i-topkhanah. Not only the artillerymen but also the musketeers were under his command. As the artillery of the Turks of Europe was much more advanced and efficient than that of the Mughal Emperors, the latter tried to get for their Mir Atish any good officer of the Turkish empire or even Persian that they could secure. On the whole the Indian Muhammadans were remarkably incompetent in handling artillery, and this department was filled with Turkish and Feringi gunners and cannon-founders, while the musketeers were mostly recruited from certain Hindu tribes, such as the Bundelas, the Karnatakis and the men of Buxar. Each field army had its own special chief of artillery.

I shall not discuss the military department any further, as it has been fully treated in William Irvine's Army of the Indian Moghuls.

§5. The Khan-i-saman or High Steward.

The High Steward was a very important officer of the Mughal times, as he was the head of the emperor's household department* and accompanied him during his journeys and campaigns. All the personal servants of the emperor were under this officer's control, and he also supervised the emperor's daily expenditure, food, tents, stores, etc. Naturally the Khan-i-saman enjoyed great trust and influence and there are examples of wazirs being appointed from among the Khan-i-samans.

---

* Manucci writes, "He had charge of the whole expenditure of the royal household in reference to both great and small things." (Storia do Mogor, ii. 419.) See, also, my History of Aurangzib iii. 79.

§6. The Judiciary.

The emperor, as "the Khalif of the Age," was theoretically the highest judge and used to hold courts of justice and try select cases personally on Wednesdays. But the court held by him was a tribunal of the highest appeal rather than a court of first instance. The Qazi was the chief judge in criminal suits and tried them according to Muslim law. Not only all cases between Muhammadans but also all-important criminal cases in which one of the parties was a Muhammadan, had to be instituted in the Qazi's court. Assisted by a mufti, who consulted the old Arabic books on jurisprudence and stated the abstract law bearing on the case, the Qazi pronounced sentence.

Naturally the great power and irresponsible position of the Qazi enabled him to turn his office into a vast field of corruption and all the Qazis of the Mughal period, with a few honourable exceptions were notorious for taking bribes. (History of Aurangzib, iii. 84-86.) The supreme Qazi of the empire was called the Qazi-ul-quzat and also "the Qazi of the imperial camp," and he always accompanied the emperor. Every provincial capital had its local Qazi, who was appointed by the Chief Qazi. These posts were often sold for bribes and the Qazi's department became a byword and reproach in Mughal times.

The following is the customary charge of the diwan to a newly appointed Qazi; "Be just, be honest, be impartial." Hold trials in the presence of the parties and at the courthouse and the seat of government (muhakuma.)

"Do not accept presents from the people of the place where you serve, nor attend entertainments given by anybody and everybody.

"Write your decrees, sale-deeds, mortgage-bonds and other legal documents very carefully, so that learned men may not pick holes in them and bring you to shame.

"Know poverty (faqr) to be your glory (fakhr)." [Manual, pp. 41-42.]

The Mufti is urged to spend his days and nights in reading books on jurisprudence and the reports of cases from which one can learn precedents. When he finds the judgment proposed in a case by the Qazi under whom he serves to be opposed to all precedent, he should tell him politely, "Sir, in a similar case, reported in such and such a book, the judgment is given thus. It would be better if you pronounce your own judgment after reading that book."

The Mufti should train himself during his leisure-hours by copying learned legal decisions and discussions of judicial principles from authoritative textbooks. [Manual, 43-44.]

The Sadr was judge and supervisor of the endowments of land made by the emperor or princes for the support of pious men, scholars, and monks. It was his duty to see that such grants were applied to the right purpose and also to scrutinise applications for fresh grants. Assistance was often given in cash also. The rent-free land granted bore the names of sayur-ghal (Turkish), madad-i-mash (Arabic), aima etc. The Sadr was also the emperor's almoner and had the spending of the vast sums which the emperors set apart for charity in the month of Ramzan and other holy occasions, —amounting to 1 $^{1}/_{2}$ lakhs of Rupees in the reign of Aurangzib and Court ceremonies. The Sadr's position offered him boundless possibilities of enriching himself by means of bribes and peculation, and the Sadrs of Akbar's reign were notorious for their venality and cruel spirit.

The Chief Sadr of the empire was called the Sadr-us-sadur, the Sadr-i-jahan, or popularly the Sadr-i-kul. In addition, every province had its local Sadr. Practically the Sadr was exclusively a civil judge but not of all civil cases. For the posts of Qazi and Sadr, men of high Arabic scholarship and reputed sanctity of character, where available, were chosen.

The Chief Sadr, when sending the provincial Sadrs to their charges, is instructed to give them lists of the recipients of rent-free lands and daily allowances in their respective provinces, and copies of the Emperor's regulations concerning the death or flight of the servitors [of the mosques], aimadars, rozinadars, students and other persons in receipt of stipends (both hereditary and new) and urge them to act according to the imperial orders. [Manual, 39-40.]

§7. The Censor of Public Morals.

According to Muslim law, it is the king's duty to appoint an Inspector or Censor of Public Morals (Muhtasib) to regulate the lives of the people in strict accordance with the scriptural rules. The Censor's functions are to enforce the Prophet's commands and put down the practices forbidden by him (amr wa nihi), —such as drinking distilled spirits and fermented beer, bhang (i.e., hemp or Cannabis sativa) and other liquid intoxicants, gambling, and certain kinds of immorality. Dry intoxicants were not condemned, and we find both opium and ganja (i.e., dried hemp plant) allowed. The punishment of heretical opinions, blasphemy against the Prophet and neglect of the five daily prayers and the fast of Ramzan by Muhammadans also lay within the province of the Censor. He used to go through the streets with a party of soldiers demolishing and plundering liquor-shops, distilleries, and gambling-dens wherever he found them, breaking with blows the pots and pans for preparing bhang and enforcing the strict observance of religious rites on the part of the Muhammadan population. Sometimes his retainers had armed conflicts with the bold sinners who showed fight. The demolition of newly built temples was one of this officer's duties in Aurangzib's reign. (History of Aurangzib, iii. 93-94, 323.)

The following instructions are given to a newly appointed Muhtasib (Censor) as to his duties: —

"To those Muhammadans who do not know the rules of worship according to the true faith and Musalmani conduct or ceremonies you should give instructions in these matters. If they plead inability, reprimand, or chastise them.

"In the bazars and lanes observe if any one, contrary to the regulations and custom, has screened off (abru) a part of the street, or closed the path, or thrown dirt and sweepings on the road,—or if any one has seized the portion of the bazar area reserved for public traffic and opened his shop there; you should in such cases urge them to remove the violation of regulations.

In the cities do not permit the sale of intoxicating drinks nor the residence of 'professional women' (tawaif, literally, dancing girls), as it is opposed to the Sacred Law.

"Give good counsel and warning to those who violate the Quranic precepts. Do not show harshness [at first], for then they would give you trouble. First send advice to the leaders of these men and if they do not listen to you then report the case to the governor." [Manual, 45-46.]

§8. Our sources of information.

I shall now describe and critically examine the original sources of information that we possess about the Mughal system of administration.

The best known of them and the one most accessible to English-speaking readers is Abul Fazl's Ain-i-Akbari of which a scholarly translation in 3 volumes by Blochmann and Jarrett is available. But this work, though it was the progenitor and in certain respects the model of later official handbooks, has many defects. It was the first work of its kind in India and was written when the newly created Mughal administration was in a half fluid condition. Abul Fazl, therefore, tells us what an officer ought to aim at doing, rather than what the experienced servants of a long-settled government were in the habit of doing; that is to say, he draws an ideal picture instead of giving us a faithful description of the administration in its actual working. Moreover, he is an insufferable rhetorician and even when he intends to tell a fact, he buries it under a mass of figures of speech and round-about expressions. His work, therefore, does not give us much real help in drawing a correct and detailed picture of the administrative machinery, though in the statistical portion he is detailed and correct. We are oppressed by a sense of the vagueness and unreality of the picture as we go through the descriptive parts of the Ain.

The immense size of the book and the unreality, or rather the practical uselessness of much of its contents, made it undesirable to write similar works or to bring the Ain-i-Akbari up to date in the reigns of Akbar's successors. The needs of their officials were met by compiling a class of handbooks called Dastur-ul-aml, written in the exact antithesis of the style of Abul Fazl. These are highly condensed abstracts, full of facts figures and lists, with no descriptive matter and hardly any complete sentence. (They remind us of the sutras or strings of short rules in the post-Vedic Sanskrit literature.) Such small handbooks could be easily revised and brought up to date in successive reigns. But the revision took the form of making additions at the end of each section, bringing the work up to date. For this reason, the latest Dastur is the one most useful to us; it includes its predecessors, and we miss only a few old statistics which have been replaced by more recent information.

Such Dastur-ul-amls were composed in the reigns of Shah Jahan and Aurangzib, and several MSS of them are known to exist. Thomas* used five of these works. I have used one of these five, (namely, D. 163 of the Asiatic Society of Bengal) along with other sources in writing My India of Aurangzib: statistics, topography, and roads (1901.)

---

* *Revenue Resources of the Mughal Empire, p. 14 and footnote, p. 33 and footnote, esp. 40 n, —I.O. L, 1387, Br. Mus, Addl. 6598 and 6599, A.S B MS. (D. 163) and another MS. Copied for Elliot.*

But a better Dastur-u-aml has since then been copied and studied by me. One MS. of it is the India Office Library (London) No. Pers. 370, which is defective at both ends and the other is the British Museum Oriental No. 1641, complete but entitled Zawabit-i'-Alamgiri, or the Regulations of the Emperor Aurangzib. The two MSS are copies of the same work, in spite of the difference in their titles and the fact that they were transcribed from different manuscripts. They give figures up to the 33rd year of that Emperor's reign, i.e., 1690 A.D., when the Mughal empire had reached its climax after the capture of Bijapur, Golkonda and Raigarh (the Maratha capital) and the annexation of these three kingdoms to the territory of Delhi. Mere statistics of a later date, down to about the middle of the 18th century, can be found in the works of Jag-jivan Das and Rai Chatar-man, the latter of which I have given in English in my India of Aurangzib. But as they do not treat of the administrative system, they must be left out of our present study.

§9. Contents of Dastur-ul-aml.

These Dastur-uUamls or official handbooks tell us, in the fewest words possible, about the revenues of the different provinces, the number of their subdivisions, the distances between different cities of the empire, the rules for sending official papers to Court, the records that should come to the different diwans offices, the total expenditure of the State, the number of mansabdars and other military forces, the usual titles of Muslim and Hindu nobles, musicians and caligraphists, the distribution of work among the bakhshis and diwans, the functions and official procedure of the Khan-i-saman Bayutat Mir Atish Mushrifs of the barqandazes and other special classes of troops, as well as of the bakhshi of the Ahadis, details of the High Diwan's office-work and the papers to be received, replied to, prepared or signed or submitted to the Emperor by him, minute rules about the cash salaries of the princes and mansabdars, the rules of branding and shoeing cavalry horses, the classification of officers according to their equipment, rules about leave and overstaying leave, minute regulations about adjusting the jagir to an officer's rank, payment of retainers, grant for the fodder of the transport cattle of the different grades of mansabdars.

Then we have tables of weights (as current in different parts), the exchange value of the coins of different countries outside India, a list of the forts in the empire, the number of the mansabdars grade by grade, rules about promotion dismissal and sick-leave—in short all kinds of salary-rules; the special salaries of European gunners, sappers and cannon-founders (Z. 60 h-62 b), powder-supply to musketeers (Z. 63 a), classification of arms, rates of jaziya, list of seasons appropriate for voyages (Z. 67 a-68 a), the revenue of Persia, the escheated properties of various princes princesses and nobles, lists of presents received from Persia, the amounts in the imperial treasure-rooms (Z. 132 b), lists of karkhanahs (Z. 132 h—133 a), lists of the abwabs abolished by Aurangzib and of the practices declared by him as illegal (Z. 135 a—137 a), details about Aurangzib's armaments at the sieges of Bijapur Golkonda, etc., with descriptions of some of the Deccan forts of his time,—and many more details about the Emperor's Deccan campaigns and statistics about his Deccan provinces.

It will be seen from the above what a vast mass of useful and absolutely new information is compressed into this Dastur-ul-aml. Without its a thorough study of the Mughal administration would have been impossible. Unfortunately, both the MSS are badly written, and in several places the minor technical official terms can be read only by conjecture; the figures too are written not in Arabic numerals but by means of peculiar signs called raqaim, which when written with the least negligence may make a difference of tenfold or hundredfold. No distinctly written old and reliable copy of the Dastur is likely to be discovered.

Hence, we cannot extract the fullest benefit from this valuable source. Part of our reading of it must be conjectural and in a few places the text must be given up as hopelessly unreadable.

Happily, in some respects we can correct and supplement the Dastur from a later work, which is unique of its kind in Indo-Persian literature. I mean the Mirat-i-Ahmadi or History of Gujrat written in 1748 by Muhammad Ali Khan, the diwan of the province. The author has given full copies of as many of the imperial farmans addressed to the officials of this province as were preserved in his office. In this respect the book is a veritable mine of accurate information based upon authentic State papers. A comparison with the versions of a few of these farmans given in other works proves the honesty and industry of Muhammad Ali Khan.

This book has been lithographed at Bombay by a man who wrote a beautiful hand, no doubt but whose knowledge of Persian historical prose was limited. He has left several gaps in the text, reproduced the mistakes of the original copy without correction and written the obscure words without any attempt to make them intelligible; —evidently, he himself did not understand them. A correct and reliable old MS. of this work, if discovered, would greatly add to our knowledge exactly where we are most in need of light.

§10. Manual of Officers' Duties.

A secondary source of information on the Mughal administration is a curious Persian manuscript, written not later than the early 18th century, which I secured from an old Kayastha family of the Patna district. It is a small book, 138 pages of 11 lines each, with the beginning, end and two leaves in the middle missing. I shall call it the Manual of the Duties of Officers.

We know that Egypt under Arab rule produced a number of works written by officials which are of the highest value to a student of administration. "Musabbihi gives a wealth of official documents……The very minute descriptions of etiquette at the Fatimid Court in Ibn Tuwair seem to be copied from a book of Court ceremonial. Ibn Mammati gives from personal knowledge rules for the diwans and later al-Omari a chancery-manual, the most perfect work on the latter's model being Kalkashandi's……Finally writers like Ibn Duknak and Ibn Dji'an use or reproduce bodily records of official surveys." (Encyclopcedia of Islam, ii. 22.)

My last-named MS. gives minute directions as to how the different officials o the Mughal government should conduct themselves, what functions they were expected to discharge, what precautions they should take, and what records they should draw up or keep in duplicate. It is in the form of a dialogue. Each section begins with the statement that an aspirant for some office (let us call it faujdari), asks an expert in the work "How should I act in-order to satisfy my master, please the people and secure good name and prosperity for myself?" He receives a reply giving a long list of the special virtues that the newly appointed functionry must practise, the exact nature of his office-work, his temptations, and dangers. A part of the reply is, no doubt, abstract or general got counsel but much of it is based on actual sentence and the long-observed practice or the Mughal administrators. Here we get an inside view of that administration which mere theoretical treatises cannot give us.

The information supplied by these sources can be supplemented from the long Court annals of the Mughal Emperors beginning with the Akbarnamah of the 16th century and ending with the Bahadur Shah-namah of 1709. But the information on changes and innovations in the administration rules or procedure given in them is diffused over a vast area and it takes a life's study through these long annals to pick the necessary facts out, piece them together and reconstruct the history of the growth of the administration through the course of two centuries. I have collected together such scattered information for a half century only namely the reign of Auangzib.

Certain other MSS. (such as the Nigar-namah-i-minshi and the Insha-i-Harkaran) give blank forns of the letters-patent appointing diwans balhshis amins and most other officers to their posts. From these we can learn the nature of the work they were expected to do.

CHAPTER III

THE TREASURY AND HOUSEHOLD DEPARTMENTS.

§1. Diwan or Chancellor of the Exchequer.

The Exchequer was presided over by the High Chancellor (Diwan-i-ala) who bore the courtesy title of wazir and had two assistants called the Diwan-i-tan (or Diwan of Salaries) and the Diwan-i-khalsa (or Diwan of Crownlands.)

The term diwan has been derived by orientalists from a hypothetical Iranian word dewan, connected with dabir, meaning 'writer'— (like the Turkish official title bitikchi which means 'writer.) The first use of the word diwan was in the sense of the public registers of receipts and expenditure kept in Greek (in Syria and Egypt) and in Pahlavi (in Persia) in the early years of Arab conquest. The name next passed to the officers of the Treasury, and thence extended to the government of the Abbasid Khalifs and in Saladin's time to the Khalif himself. (Encyclopcedia of Islam, i. 979.)

We can get a clear general idea of the High Diwan's position and duties if we bear the following facts in our mind:

(a) He was the intermediary between the emperor and the rest of the official world.

(b) Practically all official records (except those of a technical character or containing minute details) had to be sent to his office for his inspection and storage under his control. His was the Public Records Office.

(c) Abstracts of all transactions and payments in all departments (except the smallest) had to be inspected and criticised by him.

(d) No order for appointment (except that of menials, workmen and privates in the army), promotion or large payment could have effect without his written sanction.

(e) He kept in his own hands the threads of the revenue collection and expenditure in all parts of the empire and often in great detail, and the emperor kept his finger on the pulse of State finance by means of the abstracts which the diwan had to submit to him almost daily and also by frequently asking him to read the details out.

(f) Within certain limits he was given full discretion as, to what matters he should report to the emperor and take his orders on them and what matters not.

(g) He was the embodiment of the Government on the administrative side and had to give formal leave (rukhsat) to all high officers on their appointment, charge them solemnly with their duties and receive regular reports from them on the state of their provinces.

(h) The provincial diwans were constantly and minutely controlled and guided by him from the imperial Court. Revenue was his own special department and these diwans and their underlings stood in direct contact with him.

(i) His seal and signature were necessary for the validation of most papers (including copies of the emperor's writings or reports of his verbal orders) and the authentication of the true copies of nearly all official documents.

§2. Records that had to reach the Diwan's office.

Funds (tahvils) the records of which must go to the office of the diwan:

1. Those whose siaha and awarija* alike are sent to the diwan's office:

* Siaha—The daily ledger or account book of the receipts and disbursements....... specifying all sums received, whether regular or miscellaneous, and all items of disbursement, whether customary or incidental.
Awarija—An abstract account of receipts and disbursements; a rough notebook. [Wilson's Glossary, 481 and 40.]

The funds of ---

1. Servants (itba‘; or ibtia‘=sale)
2. Ahadis (gentlemen troopers)
3. Rewards (ina‘m)
4. Cash inside the mahal (female apartments)
5. The deer-park
6. Recovery of aids or advances to officers (baz-yaft-i-musa‘idat)
7. Arrears (baqaya)
8. Fines
9. Total expenditure (kharch-i-kul)
10. Cattle food (khurak-i-dawab)
11. Menial servants (shagird-pesha)
12. [Not read clearly]
13. Substitute for jagir (‘iyuz-i-jagir)
14. The lady begams
15. House-rent (kiraya)
16. Nim-gosht and pao-gosht
17. Ready money (mablaghi)
18. Advances (musa‘idat)
19. Nazar to the Emperor
20. [Not read]
21. Damage to crops (paimal-i-zara‘at)
22. The servants (khadiman) of the mahal (i.e.,harem)

II. Those funds whose siaha is not sent but only the awarija, to the Diwan's office:

1. The butler's department (abdar-khanah)

2. Articles in the Octagonal tower [of Agra fort.]

3. Asbab-i-mahlaghi

4. [Text illegible]

5. Ewer-holder's department (aftabchi-khanah)

6. Blacksmith's department

7. Cook's department, with four branches

8. Bedding (basta khdnah)

9. Betel-leaf department. —(a) betel-leaf and (b) vessels for the same

10. Bhanda-khanah

11. [Text illegible]

12. China-ware department

13. Charandhari khanah (?)†

14. Leather goods department

15. Chapel (ja-namaz khanah)

16. Butcher's department

17. Charkhi-khanah? (spindles)

18. Scents

† Charhandar—a servant accompanying a cargo of goods; a supercargo. (Wilson, 103)

19. Palace buildings

20. Fodder of oxen

21. Fodder of camels [text reads tigers]

22. Department for setting shells (Khatam bandi khanah)

23. Covers of trays of the food department

24. Balance room (dandi-khanah)

25. Cauldron department, copper vessels

26. Tray department

27. Gold embroidery department

28. Saddle department

29. [Text illegible]

30. Sukh-sajya*

31. Trappings (rakhwat) department with four branches, —(a) trappings for leopards, (b) for elephants, (c) for haveli and (d) for bárish-khánah (monsoon house)

32. Lamps of the light department

33. Sharbat khanah

34. Sandalwood-ware department

35. Plate and saucers, consisting of (a)

---

* Sukh-sajya is a Sanskrit word meaning 'cosy bed'. The Ain-i-Akbari (ii. 122) describes a sukh-asan (or cosy litter) used by the rich men of Bengal in travelling.

III.] ABSTRACT ACCOUNTS TO BE SENT.

(a) goldware, (b) silverware, (c) damascened-ware and (d) Kar-karaqi

36. [Text doubtful, either the food or the giltware department]

37. Standard and arms department, the cash of the branches of (a) standards, (b) swords, (c)? and (d) spears.

38. Library

39. Gongs (ghariali)

40. Torches

41. Earthen pots

42. Fruits

43. Sadanand [ganja or any other special intoxicant]

44. Pictures

45. Silverware

46. Food of the [hunting] leopards.

[Z. 13b—14b.]

§3. Individual diwans' modes of transacting business.

We can get a clear idea of the High Diwan's office-work and method of transacting business from the recorded practice of some of the famous diwans of the middle of the 17th century. (D. 101 a—102 a.) Sadullah Khan (the famous wazir of Shah Jahan) used to proceed in the following way: —

First: he read the letters received and replied to them. Then he selected the applications of the tankha department which were fit to be accepted and submitted them to the emperor with reasons for their acceptance, after signing his name at the bottom. Next, the papers of the department of rent-free land grant (aima) were signed. Thereafter the abstract memos (yad-dasht) of the amin's office were signed by him. Finally, he gave a hearing to the plaintiffs. Before leaving office, he used to listen to the agents (of the princes, governors, and other nobles) who pressed their requests.

The distribution-list of the chauki (i.e., mounting guard round the palace on different nights by different nobles), was signed by him in the morning before all other work.

He used to draft the royal letters in private but urgent ones were composed by him in his office room.

Jafar Khan's office-procedure was the following: —First, he drafted the farmans and urgent letters. Then he read the papers of the tankha office, applications (arzi) and orders (parwanahs.) Next, he immediately took into consideration any paper of the Khalsa department or any naqdi or abstractmemo, etc. that anyone submitted to him, disposed of it, and applied himself to other business.

Between the death of Sadullah Khan (7th April 1656, O.S.) and the installation of Mir Jumla as his successor (July 1656), Raja Raghunath was the acting diwan. He used to conduct the work of the Exchequer thus:—

He reported to the emperor the purport of the petitions received, in the same manner as the High Diwan and then placed the papers before His Majesty. After drafting the royal letters (farmans) he submitted them to the emperor, after whose approval they were written out fair. On the attested copies (tasdiqat) of the letters (risalah) of the [provincial?] diwan, — according to which the abstract memo was drawn up, —he used to write, 'Incorporate with the report of events (waqia.)' On the abstract memos of the waqia he wrote, 'Bring to His Majesty's ears a second time (arz-i-mukarrar for confirmation) and compare with the original waqia.'

On the abstracts of waqia, —according to which the farmans were written, —he wrote 'Write an imperial farman [on the subject.]' He put his signature on the sidha of jagirs and the daul* of cash tankha, on the settlements of accounts (muhasibat), on the parwanahs of all offices, on the attested copies of the aima of the Crownland office, on the letters (arzi) from the treasuries, on the permits (dastaks) for tankha in cash and also affixed his seal to the last-mentioned papers.

His seal was impressed on the rooms of the Public Treasury and the bags of money [in them], on the abstracts of the reports (waqia), on the acknowledgments (qabz) of the monthly salary of the ahadis barqandazes and menial servants, on the sheets of the reports from the provinces which the news-letter-reader at the imperial Court after reading them to His Majesty used to send to the imperial Record Office, on the slips (nuskha)'† of the provinces sent by the [provincial] diwan or other officers.

---

*Daul—an estimate of the amount of revenue which a district or estate may be expected to yield, valuation. (Wilson. 129.)

† Nuskha—a copy, a specimen or draught of a writing &c. (Wilson, 381.)

Krori—the collector of a revenue area yielding one kror of dam, i.e., 2½ lakhs of Rupees. The office was instituted by Akbar but the jurisdiction of a krori soon lost all relation to the above amount of revenue.

On farmans he wrote 'Enter in the book' (sabat numaid.)

§4. Duties of the Diwan of Crownlands.

So much for the High Diwan. The duties of the Diwan of Crownlands (khalsa) were the following [D, 87 b; Z. 30 b]: —

The posting of the subahdars, faujdars, amins, diwani officers, kroris, and daroghas of the provinces,—of the amins, mushrifs and tahvildars of mahals,—of the fotahdars, clerks of issue (bar-amad-navisan), daroghas, amins, mushrifs and khazanchis of [provincial] treasuries,— of the sazawals of papers,—the amins and kroris of arrears,—the collectors of the mutaliba (recovery of loans or advances made by Government) and [the dues from] the zamindars.

On parwanahs the High Diwan should write 'correct' (sad) and the Diwan of Khalsa should write 'seen' (mulahiza shud).

Mushrif—an examiner (of accounts), i.e, auditor; an officer of the treasury who authenticates accounts and documents. (Wilson, 358.)

Fotahdar—a cash-keeper, a moneychanger, an officer in public establishments for weighing money and bullion and examining and valuing coins. (Wilson, 160.)

Sazawal— a bailiff or agent appointed to compel payment or attendance; an officer specially appointed to take charge of and collect the revenue of an estate from the management of which the owner or farmer has been removed. (Wilson, 473.)

Among the duties of the Diwan of Khalsa were to answer the inquiries of the lower officials ('amal'); to issue letters-patent (sanad) for services; to issue orders (parwanahs) on the parganahs assigning the cash salary (tankha) of the Emperor's sons and grandsons, according to the daul prepared by the cash department [of the Treasury];—also parwanahs for the recovery of Government advances, for the payment of the fixed salaries of the servants (ahal-i-khidmat), the customary commission of the fotahdars and the collection fee of the kroris;—parwanahs on complaints,—for the attachment [of property or crops] for unpaid arrears,—for calling up money from the [subordinate] treasuries,—for cash assignment in payment of things ordered to be manufactured [for the State, farmaish] and whatever is ordered on the provinces and troops, —for investigating any matter reported in the news-letters ;—to write letters by order (hasb-ul-hukm) on any subject as desired by the Emperor;—to issue permits (dastak) addressed to the clerks (mutasaddi) of the treasuries about the fixed tarikha which might be ordered to be paid out of the Public Treasury (i.e., the Central Treasury?),—permits addressed to the khazanchis about the tankha that may be ordered on [sub] treasuries and the troops,—passports for roads, passes for workmen.

The Diwan of Khalsa was left free to report to the emperor the summary of the despatches of the lower diwani officers at his discretion, and to reply to those that required reply. The other despatches were to be initialled by him without reporting to the emperor.

Then we have lists of the papers which had to be read to the Emperor by this Diwan and of those that had to be merely initialled by him without submission to his master. Even in the case of the former class, the Diwan could withhold unimportant papers if he thought fit. He had also to report to His Majesty the cash balances of the treasuries very frequently and the doings of the zamindars.

All parwanahs for cash payment in the imperial Household department were issued by the khan-i-saman and the Diwan merely endorsed them.

The Diwan of Khalsa had to endorse the security-bonds (tamassuk-i-zamini) of the workmen and for the repayment of State loans (mutaliba) and the indemnity-bonds (muchilka) signed by certain officers binding themselves to carry out certain specified tasks on pain of fine.

Reports from the fotahdars and khazanchis of the parganahs and provinces stating the amounts they had recovered from the loans or advances made by Government, [had to be read by the Diwan of Khalsa.]

The High Diwan should write 'sanctioned' (manzur shud) and the Diwan of Khalsa 'seen on the badar-navisi* of the amlas in the Khalsa office.

The High Diwan should write 'entrust to such and such a fund' (tahvil-i-falan numaid) on the audit-reports that are brought [to him] for signature by the mustaufis viz,, the mustaufis of revenue [or of the amlas, variant] , the mustaufi of ras-ul-mal (= trading stock or the original prices of articles), the mustaufi of treasuries, the mustaufis of arrears, the mustaufi of amual [attached property of officers who died indebted to Government], and the mustaufi of jaziya. He should also sign the attestation copy of the fixed salaries of workmen.

---

* Badar-navisi—writing off items of an account which are objectionable or excessive, audit of an account. (Wilson, 43.)

Mustaufi—an examiner or auditor of accounts; the principal officer of the department in which the accounts of ex-collectors or farmers of the revenue were examined. (Ibid, 358.)

The High Diwan should sign the sheets of the abstracts (zimn)* of imperial farmans and the Diwan of Khalsa should sign the sheets of the abstracts of diwani, faujdari and amini works (khidmat.)

The siaha of ahkam (imperial orders in writing) should be sent directly to the offices of the High Bakhshis and the Khan-i-saman.

The duties of the Diwan of Khalsa include—investigation into the notes (nuskha) of the revenue department, —correction of the tumar-i-jama (record of total standard assessment) of the Crownlands, estimating (bar-awardan) the expenditure of the troops accompanying the emperor.

The facts about dismissed officers, compiled from the office records, should be initialled by the High Diwan. An attested copy of it should be sent to the officer concerned and the sidha to the offices of the High Bakhshi &c.

The Diwan of Khalsa drew up the statement of the income and disbursement of the imperial camp and of all the subahs and kept the records of the tankha (allowances) of the Begams and lists of the mahals (villages) of the Crownlands, workmen and annual lists (?=statistical abstracts?)

---

* Zimn—the endorsement of a grant giving an abstract of its contents. Formerly the words zimn navisand 'let them write the abstract' were inscribed upon a sanad granting an assignment of revenue, which served as authority for the subordinate officers to make out the particulars of the grant. (Wilson, 567.)

The High Diwan's office kept copies of all sheets signed by the emperor.

Then we have a long list of the papers which the Diwan of Khalsa had to secure from different classes of officials, such as revenue officers, amins, kroris, collectors of sair mahals, clerks of the treasuries, as well as reports of pandit-khanah, &c.

§5. Duties of the Diwan of Tankha.

The Diwan-i-tan dealt with the following matters [Z. 34 b—36 a; D. 89 b—90 b]:

(A) Requiring submission to the emperor:

Whatever appertained to the subjects of jagirs and cash tankha. Facts relating to iamindars.

Daul of the jagirs of subahdars.

Records of arrears.

Awarija of the parganahs.

Taujih of jagirdars.

Ranks of the mansabdars.

(B) Orders (parwanahs) relating to the granting (tankha) of jagir, cash salary, fixed salaries of workmen and the people of the tahvils, —on complaints and investigation of the sheets of news-letters—orders for the attachment of jagirs [in the case of officers who] have been transferred from a parganah, —orders for the recovery of advances made to mansabdars.

(C) Sheets to be signed—the siaha of jagirs, the grant of aid (musa'idat), sheets of the demand for the restitution of advances, questions.

(D) Permits (dastaks) for grant (tankha) of cash and grant of aid.

(E) After the Emperor had signed the tumars of arrears and of officers entitled to pay (talbdar), the High Diwan should copy the emperor's words (i.e., writing) on these papers and sign them. Imperial orders in writing (ahkam) should be sent immediately to the offices of the Bakhshi and others. The Diwan should sign the audit-reports [or settlements of accounts] submitted by the various mustaufis.

The daul of cash payment should be signed by the Diwan-i-tan. On the sheets of 'branding and verification of cavalry' he should write 'sanctioned.'

On the abstract memos of the salaries of workmen he should write 'From such a date in such a year pay cash tankha.'

On the memos of the mansabdars and others [he should write] 'Bring to the Emperor's notice a second time, for confirmation and truly compare [with the original.]'

(F) Aima and other things—farmans, memos, parwanahs for grant of help to living (madad-i-mash,) Keep the newsletters of the provinces, &c. in [your] office.

(G) The writing office—farmans in terms of the emperor's dictation, —parwanahs 'by order' (hasb-ul-hukm).

§6. Duties of the High Steward.

The Khan-i-saman or High Steward, as I have already pointed out, was the second highest officer in the realm and stood immediately below the Diwan. He has been well described as "really the diwan of expenditure." (Manual, 15.)

He is thus instructed about his work, [Manual, 15—19]: —

"Take over the cash balance and collected articles in the Household Department, which are kept under the seals of the late Khan-i-saman at the time of his vacating his office and the seals of the mushrif and tahvildar; satisfy yourself that the stock agrees with the records or else call upon them to make the deficit good.

"Keep with yourself one set of the records of expenditure per annum arranged under the heads of the different karkhanahs (i.e., stores and State factories). Find out how many khilats (robes) are there in the khilat-khanah and so on in every karkhanah. If the requisite stores are wanting, write out a statement of the expenditure (saranjam) necessary for supplying the want, apply to the proper authority, take from him a tankha on the diwan for the saranjam and make the things.

In order that the Khan-i-saman may be in a position to supply all articles that may be required, it is his business to buy them with Government money or on credit from traders and keep them ready and deliver them to Government at need at the market price. If he is a rich man himself, he ought to buy and stock the things, so that he may not have to beg of others at the time of need but issue them after valuation at the market rate. Thus, his master will have no occasion to be displeased at delay in supplying. If the Khan-i-saman supplies his own things at the market rate, most probably Government will make a saving by the transaction; but the clerks of the Government will allege that he is selling things to the State at a profit; therefore, he ought to ask the Emperor beforehand to advance him money to buy everything and stock it for supply when needed.

"Old and secondhand stores should be sold to the army after taking permission [of the emperor] and learning their current prices from a muqim [=broker or appraiser.] Keep the pricelist, signed by the muqim, with yourself [for your defence.]

"Buy beautiful things which are likely to prove agreeable [to the emperor] and keep them [for presentation on suitable occasions.] On the two Ids and other festive occasions, keep the robes [of honour] and other customary official gifts ready [for issue] a month or two before the dates, so that you may not have to plead inability to supply when they are needed.

"Treat well and attach to yourself by the ties of gratitude artisans like goldsmiths, enamellers, die-carvers [for coins], net-weavers, plain workers on metal [sdcah kar, a class of goldsmiths], &c., &c."

The duties of a Khan-i-saman are thus enumerated in the Dastur: —

(1) Attestation [of the salary-bills] of the workmen and menials from the monthly, yearly, and daily rolls [of attendance] of those newly appointed as well as increment [in the salary] of the old ones.

(2) First appointment, dismissal and posting of daroghas, amins, mushrifs and tahvildars [of the various karkhanahs.]

(3) Laying down rules for the work of the karkhanahs and treasuries [of the Household department.]

(4) [Writing] slips for hire and wages of labour.

(5) Replying to the prayers of the managers of the karkhanahs.

(6) Issuing permits for reward and (?) for taking possession of houses. [Doubtful.]

(7) Inspection of the half-meat and quarter-meat [dishes.]

(8) Taking bonds for money security from the menials and managers [of karkhanahs.]

(9) Considering applications from the workshops and stores.

(10) Taking care of the nazar, charity fund and presents.

(11) Fixing the daily rations of cattle.

(12) Permits for the loan of articles from the karkhanahs.

(13) Permits for the distribution of food (increase or decrease) and the letters of order (ahkam), —except the letters of the female apartments. These were to be signed first by the Khan-i-saman and then by the Bayutat.

(14) Reply to the final presentation of accounts (muhasibat) concerning the recovery of State advances (mutalibat.)

(15) Escheat of property. If the order is to restore [to the officer under audit], then send a copy of the order to the office [of the Diwan?], so that his tankha may be paid according to it.

(16) Things ordered (farmaish) by the emperor from the provinces.

(17) Taking the income from the gardens and the rent from the shops and residential houses [belonging to the State.]

(18) Long sheets of letters from the karkhanahs.

(19) The daily accounts and awarijah of the subahs as well as the awarijah of the imperial camp are to be sealed without change.

(20) Initial the petitions from the officers asking for advances and the granting of residences to alight in, &c.

(21) Attestation of the attendance of the daroghas, amins, mushrifs and tahvildars of karkhanahs.

(22) Appraising the different articles of peshkash (tribute and present) and amual (escheated personal property of dead mansabdars.)

(23) Attestation of the cash reward which appertains to the commander of the squadron (sahib-i-risalah)?

(24) Distribution of porters among the different karkhanahs.

(25) Arrangements for the marriages of the princes.

(26) The tumars (registers) of the cash realisation of the amounts due on audit (muhasibat), should be sent by the auditors to the office of the Khan-i-saman and a copy of them should be given to the office of the Bayutat.

(27) Plans of lodgings and buildings [intended to be constructed for the State?]

[Z. 20 a-21b; D. 83 a-84 a.]

§7. Duties of the Bayutat.

The Bayutat. —This name is derived from the Arabic word bait, meaning 'house'. In Mughal India it was the title of an officer who registered the property of deceased persons, in order to secure the payment of the dues of the State as well as to safeguard the property for the heirs of the deceased. In addition, he was in some respects an understudy of the Khan-i-saman, as the following list of his duties [Z. 21 b; D. 84 a] will show: —

(1) To allot money to the various funds or cash balances out of the general treasury of expenditure and karkhanahs.

(2) To escheat the property of deceased nobles in co-operation with the Khan-i-saman.

(3) To make provisions (saranjam) for the karkhanahs.

(4) [To fix] the prices of articles.

(5) Estimating the [necessary] treasury of the karkhanahs. Send the estimate of the monthly expenditure to the Diwan's office.

(6) Daily accounts of the karkhanahs accompanying: the emperor during his marches.

(7) Holding receipts (qabuz) in trust.

(8) The Bayutat should write the date on the descriptive rolls (chihra) of the menials.

(9) On the report of branding of cattle, he should write "Brought to the branding."

(10) [Rejection or sale of] old articles in the karkhanahs, according to the suggestions received from each of the latter.

(11) Fixing residences for the cattle.

(12) Siaha of tankha from the expenditure treasury. The advance to the menials barqandazes and cattle should be made by the bayutat himself.

(13) The slips (chithi) granting articles (jins wa ajnas) should be kept in the office of the bayutat.

(14) The rooms of the karkhanahs should be sealed with the bayutat's seal.

(15) Grant [to] petty officials for foodstore (zakhira.)

(16) Assessment of the prices of the things in the 'sale' department and [keeping] the cash under the seal of the bayutat.

(17) The requisitions of the karkhanahs to be signed first by the bayutat and then by the Khan-i-saman.

(18) The siaha of the expenditure and the summary grant (sarasari tankha) for food to the cattle should go to the bayutat's office and there after be signed by the Khan-i-saman.

CHAPTER IV

PROVINCIAL ADMINISTRATION.

§ 1. Official dislike of village life and indifference to village interests.

The administrative agency in the provinces of the Mughal empire was an exact miniature of that of the Central Government. There was the governor (officially styled the nazim and popularly called the subahdar), the diwan, the bakhshi, the qazi, the sadr and the censor but no Khan-i-saman and no bayutat. These provincial bakhshis were really officers attached to the contingents that accompanied the different subahdars rather than officers of the subahs as geographical units. The practical effect, however, was the same.

The administration was concentrated in the provincial capital. It was city-government, not in the Greek sense of the term but rather as a government living and working in cities and mainly concerning itself with the inhabitants of the cities and their immediate neighbourhood. the Mughals, —after due allowance has been made for their love of hunting and laying out pleasure gardens and their frequent marches, — were essentially an urban people in India and so were their courtiers, officials and generally speaking the upper and middle classes of the Muhammadan population here. The villages were neglected and despised and village-life was dreaded by them as a punishment. No doubt, the villages were the places from which their food and income came; but that was their only connection with them. Life in a village was as intolerable to them as residence on 'the Getic and Sarmatian shores' away from 'the seat of empire and of the gods' was to a cultured poet of imperial Rome. This feeling comes out very clearly in a Persian couplet:

Zagh dum su-i-shahar wa sar su-i-deh

Dum-i-an zagh az sar-i-u beh.*

The tail of a crow was turned towards the city,

and its head towards the village;

Surely, the tail here was better than the head!

'Better, i.e., nobler, or happier.

---

* Hamiduddin's Ahkam-i-Alarmgiri, p. 33 of the text as published by me.

The provincial Government kept touch with the villages by means of

(1) the faujdars posted to the sub-divisions, who almost always lived in the lesser towns

(2) the lower officials of the revenue department, who did the actual collection from the peasantry

(3) the visits of the zamindars to the subahdar's court and

(4) the tours of the subahdar. The contact, however, was not very intimate and the villagers, as I have remarked in the first lecture were left pretty much to their own devices, uninfluenced by and indifferent to the Government at the chief town of the province, so long as they paid the land-tax and did not disturb the peace.

§2. The subahdar and his duties.

The term SUBAHDAR comes from the Arabic word sub meaning direction or point of the compass. In very early times the provinces into which every large kingdom was necessarily divided were named in accordance with their bearings towards the capital, —such as the viceroyalty of the north, of the south, of the east and of the west, —in whichever of these directions there was enough territory to compose a separate province. Similarly, the provincial governors of the Bahmani empire were styled tarf-dars from the word tarf meaning direction.

With the country covered by an immense number of small geographical units, each occupied by a different tribe and the tribes often migrating from place to place, it was at first impossible to give any single historical or tribal name to a province, which was the aggregate of several such tribal settlements and socially unconnected districts. It was more convenient to designate the viceroyalties as the northern, the southern, &c. Hence, the origin of the terms subahdar and tarfdar.

The subahdar was officially called the nazim or regulator of the province. His essential duties were to maintain order, to help the smooth and successful collection of revenue and to execute the royal decrees and regulations sent to him.

When a newly appointed subahdar went to the High Diwan to take his leave before setting out for his province, the Diwan was to deliver the following charge to him:

"Experienced men have written concerning a subahdar's work that he ought to keep all classes of men pleased by good behaviour and to see that the strong may not oppress the weak. He should keep all oppressors down, &c.

"A subahdar's recommendations about the mansabdars under him are naturally valued and given effect to by his sovereign and therefore the subahdar should take care to recommend only worthy officials for promotion. He should punish rebellious zamindars and all lawless men and every month send two despatches to Court by dak chauki reporting the occurrences of the province.

"He should never release robbers by taking anything from them because this practice amounts to 'sowing the seed of oppression', as other rich men, knowing that they can secure impunity by giving bribes, will practise very great tyranny, so that it will in the end be very difficult for you to control them." [Manual, 11 - 12]

A new viceroy is instructed about his work thus [Manual, 25-30]: —

"When you are appointed, you should engage a good diwan, —a trustworthy and experienced man who has already done work in the service of some high grandee, —and a munshi (secretary) with similar ability and experience. You should secure a trustworthy mediator or friend (wasilah) at Court to report promptly to the emperor and take his orders on any affair of the province on which you may write to His Majesty. To this mediator you will have to give presents, for such is the usage of our times. When people visit the tombs of dead saints, they offer flowers and sweetmeats for gaining their favours. How much more are presents necessary for gaining the favour of living men!!!

"Learn from the well-informed men of the province how many of the zamindars require the display of force and the general character of the peasants and get an estimate as to the number of sehbandi troops [i, e., irregulars employed to assist in revenue collection etc., somewhat like the armed police], necessary for doing the work of control and administration (rabt and zabt.) If you find your retainers (tabinan) and sehbandi insufficient and in other matters also require the emperor's sanction and help, then make a petition and submit it through your mediator at Court. If the Emperor grants the force that you consider necessary for the efficient management of the subah, well and good. Otherwise, if you think that you can govern the subah at your own expense and recover your costs during your tenure of office [from your salary and allowances] after getting the province under control, then do it. If not, decline the post, for what can a single trooper do? (i.e., you are only one man, if your master will not give you an adequate force.)

"When you start from the imperial capital to go to your province after your appointment enlist one-fourth of the number of tabindn (armed followers) sanctioned for you by Government; they should be good soldiers, men of good families and experienced in war. Half-way to your subah enlist one-fourth more of the same class as before. Take with yourself able and experienced candidates for [civil] offices, telling them that their service would begin from the day of your arrival at the frontier of your province. Keep half of these [prospective officers] with yourself and send the other half of the tabindn already enlisted and present with you, to the province to arrive there before you, telling them to assemble the well-informed local men and learn from them the character of every zamindar and jama'dar of the place and report to you their mutual relations and their conduct towards former subahdars as regards the payment of revenu, and how much a particular zamindar used to pay over and above the revenue. When you are still a quarter of the way from your province, send off expert troopers with your parwanahs calling upon the zamindars to wait on you at an appointed place immediately after your arrival.*

---

* E.g the practice of the subahdar of Orissa, as described by me from his letters, in my Studies in Mughal India, 206—214

"When you reach the frontier of your subah, enlist the candidates for office from that date and treat them well because their first impressions will determine their future opinion of you as a master.

"Chastise the refractory zamindars and the leaders of lawless men, so that others of the same class may take warning from it and pay revenue [without trouble.]

"Then enter the fort.* Dismiss the troops that you find unnecessary after making a survey of the situation. [Remember that] it is difficult to pay the arrears of the salaries of subordinates. Tell the diwan to spend according to the income of the province.

"Encourage the ryots to extend the cultivation and carry on agriculture with all their heart. Do not screw everything out of them. Remember that the ryots are permanent (i.e., the only permanent source of income to the State.) Conciliate the zamindars with presents; it is cheaper to keep them in hand thus than to repress them with troops!

*The fort in the chief town of the province was the subahdar's official residence and court. He entered it for the first time with much ceremony, on an auspicious day and hour chosen by his astrologers, for which the newly arrived subahdar had often to wait for weeks in a garden outside the city!

"Do not lay your hands on the villages of the Crownland (khalsa mahals), as in that case you will provoke a quarrel with the diwan of khalsa, who will complain to the emperor, and you will be called upon to explain your conduct.

"Cherish the Shaikhs and qazis. As for the darvishes who do not go to any one's house [to beg alms], inquire how they are fairing and support them with and kind. Give alms to faqirs and [ordinary] beggars. See that the strong may not oppress the weak."

Another of his duties was to collect the due tribute from vassal princes close to his jurisdiction and to arrange for its safe convoy to the imperial Court. (Studies in Mughal India, 215.)

§3. Duties of the provincial diwan.

The provincial DIWAN was the second officer in the locality and, as I have pointed out in my first lecture, he was the rival of the subahdar. The two had to keep a strict and jealous watch on each other, thus continuing the earliest administrative policy and traditions of the Arabs when they went forth after the Prophet's death, conquering the world and establishing their new government in the annexed lands.

The provincial diwan was selected by the Imperial Diwan and acted directly under his orders and in constant correspondence with him. At the time of giving leave to a new diwan, the High Diwan was to urge him to increase the cultivation and to select honest men only for the post of amin. He was to report to the High Diwan twice every month the occurrences of the subah with a statement of the cash balance with him. The diwan was specially urged to appoint as collectors (kroris and tahsildars) practical men who were likely to induce the ryots to pay the Government due of their own accord without the necessity of resorting to harshness or chastisement. [Manual, 12—13.]

The sanad or letter of appointment of a provincial diwan charges him with his duties in the following words: —

"Cause the extension of cultivation and habitation in the villages. Watch over the imperial treasury, that nobody may draw any money without due warrant. When due money is paid into the treasury from the chests of the fotahdars and other sources, give receipts (qabz-ul-wasul) to their agents. See that no official exacts any forbidden cess (abwab.)

"At the end of every agricultural season ascertain from the original rough papers [i.e., first notes] the extortions and peculations of the 'amils and recover for the imperial treasury whatever may be due from them on this account. Report bad or dishonest amils to Government [i.e., to the High Diwan] so that better men may be appointed to replace them.

"If any amil has let arrears [of revenue] accumulate for many years, you should collect the due amount from the villages in question by easy instalments at the rate of 5 p. c. every season.

"The taqavi loan given last year by Government should be realised in the first season of the present year. If they fail to pay or delay payment,

Government will compel the diwan and the amin to make the amount good.

"Send the papers of your department to the imperial record office according to the regulations."*

---

* Some of these regulations are given in Aurangzib's farman to Rasik-das, which I have translated into English in my Studies in Mughal India, 196—197.

§4. The faujdar and his functions.

In the maintenance of peace and the discharge of executive functions in general, the subahdar's assistants were the FAUJDARS. These officers were placed in charge of suitable subdivisions of the province, provided that they were sufficiently civilised or important on account of the presence of zamindars or large sources of State revenue in them and also if they contained towns. Thus, among the faujdaris of the subah of Bihar were (1) Palamau, (2) Darbhanga or Tirhut and (3) Hajipur. As for Mungir and Bhagalpur, I have found no precise mention of them as seats of faujdars in the 17th century Persian records. In Bengal, Hughli, Jessore, Gauhati, Sylhet, Medinipur and probably also Ghoraghat, were among the faujdari divisions.

When a new faujdar was appointed, he was given the following advice as to his policy and conduct: —

"A faujdar should be brave and polite in dealing with his soldiers. He should enlist in his contingent of armed retainers only men of known bravery and good family.

"As soon as you reach the place of your service, find out the people who knew the pass administration of the locality, viz,, the qanungoes and others, win their hearts and learn from them which of the troops quartered in your subdivision are inclined to take advantage of their commander's weakness or the difficulties of the administration and which of them are in secret league with the lawless zamindars.

"Learn whether the local zamindars paid the revenue regularly or displayed a defiant spirit in your predecessor's time. In the case of zamindars who are not naturally disposed to be submissive, first treat them well and if they do not respond by offering obedience, then chastise them. When your own troops are insufficient to crush such a refractory zamindar, set his enemies up against him, make a grant of this zamindar 's lands to his rival and send your own troops to co-operate with those of the rival in order to crush the rebel more easily.

"Arrange with a trusty clerk of the imperial Court to receive letters from you and on the basis of the information thus supplied, to report on your affairs to the Court [evidently the High Diwan.]

"Conciliate the local waqai-navis, sawanih-niqar and harkarah (i.e., the official news reporters and spies), in order that they may always write their reports of occurrences in a manner leading to your advancement.

"Keep up your practice in the exercise of all weapons of war, in hunting [mimic war] and in riding horses, so as to keep yourself in a fit condition and to be able to take the field promptly [when called upon to march to a scene of disturbance.] Do justice to the oppressed." [Manual, 32-34.]

The faujdar's duties are fully enumerated in the following sanad or letter-patent appointing him to his office: —

"Destroy the forts of lawless men and rebel chiefs as the [best] means of punishing them. Guard the roads, to protect the revenue-payers, Assist and give [armed] support to the agents (gumashtahs) of the jagirdars [in the case of military fiefs] and the kroris [in the case of Crownlands], at the time of collecting the revenue.

"Forbid the blacksmiths to manufacture matchlocks. Urge the thanahdars [men in command of the outposts or smaller areas within a faujdari], whom you appoint under yourself, to take complete possession of their charges to abstain from dispossessing people from their rightful property and from levying any forbidden cess (abwah).

"So long as the agent of the jagirdar or the amil of the Crownlands does not give you a written requisition for military aid, do not attack any village in your jurisdiction. After you have received such a requisition [or rather complaint against a defaulting and refractory village], contrive to influence some of the leading men of the village who are the sources of the trouble and try to reform them, so that they may repent of their violent and lawless conduct and incline to the payment of revenue and the peaceful pursuit of agriculture. In case they reform themselves, take a deed of agreement [to such a course] from the amil. If they refuse to reform, then chastise the evil men of the village [z.e., the ringleaders] but do not molest the [ordinary] peasants. "Guard the roads, cut the jungles, demolish the [illegal] forts, &c."

In short, the faujdar, as his name means, was only the commander of a military force stationed in the country to put down smaller rebellions, disperse or Eirrest robber-gangs, take cognisance of all violent crimes and make demonstrations of force to overawe opposition to the revenue authorities or the criminal judge or the Censor. [His functions are briefly described in Ain, I I. 40—41.]

§5. The hptwal and his duties.

In connection with the public peace, we may most conveniently discuss the kotwal and his functions here. He was essentially an urban officer, being the chief of the city police.

The ideal KOTWAL is described as a man who follows the regulations in his outward actions and fears God inwardly. He should attend when the sovereign or provincial viceroy holds a court of justice or grants public audience. On taking over charge, he should satisfy himself by a personal inspection that the horse and foot attached to his post are really up to the fixed strength and have their proper equipment, arms, and stores and that the appurtenances of his office, —such as long rods, chains, and quivers (? jaulana), —are really of the number entered in the official list. He should check the number of the persons in the prison and ascertain [their] explanation (kaifiat) of the charges against them. Then he should report to his official superior the cases of those prisoners whom he considers innocent and secure their liberation. In the case of the guilty persons who could pay, he should take orders for exacting suitable fines from them and then releasing them. In the case of penniless prisoners, the kotwal should report and act as commanded. A statement of the cases of those deserving to be kept in prison should be sent to the officers of Canon Law, and the orders passed by the latter over their signatures should be carried out by the kotwal. In the case of those deserving death, the kotwal should, through proper officers, freely state their cases to the judge (in writing) on the day of trial, receive the qazi's signed sentence of death and execute the sentence.

Summoning the watchmen and sweepers, he should take bonds from them that they should daily report to him the occurrences of every mahalla (ward of the city) without suppression or exaggeration. He should enlist a footman (piada) singly from each ward and post him there as a spy to report all news, so that he may compare the reports from these two sources and thus know the truth and do the needful in the case.

"Do justice, that the people may liken you to a qazi in the power of arriving at the truth of a case. On the public streets of the cities, post careful men to act as watchmen from sunset to 9 P.M, and 9 P.M, to dawn, to scrutinise the wayfarers and arrest those whom they consider to be thieves and evil-doers and bring them to you.

"At places of sale and purchase, at places of entertainment (shadi) where spectators assemble, keep watchmen to seize the pickpockets and the snatchers-up of things and bring them to you for punishment.

"Summoning the 'professional women', dancing-girls, liquor-sellers, and vendors of intoxicants, take bonds from them that if they do any forbidden act they would pay so much as fine. Fine them if they break the bond. At midnight take horse with your followers and patrol round the city and in the streets also. In the lanes where you had previously sent your spies and they have found dens of thieves; you should go in time and nip their mischievous designs in the bud.

"Watch and guard the prisoners very carefully lest any of them should escape." (Manual, 65—69.)

The kotwal's functions are also minutely enumerated in the Ain-i-Akbari (ii. 41—43.) But most of Akbar's regulations which this officer is there directed to enforce were withdrawn after that Emperor's death and the entire passage in the A in also seems to me to point out only the ideal for a kotwal and not to represent the actual state of things. Only, a perfect man can satisfy what is demanded of I the kotwal here. I, therefore, do not attach any value to this source.

Manucci (ii. 420—421) gives a; more valuable account of the kotwal's work from actual observation. "It is his business to stop the distillation of spirits. He has to see that there were no public women in the town, nor anything else forbidden by the king [Aurangzib.] He obtains information about all that goes in, so as to be able to send in his report [to the ruler.] For this purpose, there are throughout the Mughal empire certain persons known as halal-khor (i.e., house scavengers.) These men are under obligation to go twice a day to clean out every house and they tell the kotwal all that goes on......He also has the duty of arresting thieves and criminals. He is subordinate to the qazi and receives orders from him...Under his orders there is a considerable body of cavalry and a great number of foot soldiers; for in every ward there is a horseman and 20 to 30 foot-soldiers, who, in a sort of way, go the rounds." In a sanad of appointment the kotwal is urged to see that there may be no theft in his city and that the people of the place may enjoy security and ply their trade peacefully. He is to carry out the qazi's written orders and not to act at his own discretion in keeping men accused of peculation in prison or in releasing them. If there is a ferry at the city, he should take care not to collect any toll on the ferries (as they were abolished by the emperor) to prevent the boatmen from charging more than the proper line, and to stop lawless men and oppressors from crossing the ferries.

There was a platform (chabutra) in front of the kotwal's office and bordering the public road, where malefactors were often exhibited.

§6. News-reporters.

The agency by which the central Government, learnt the news of the country consisted of the waqai-navis, (2) the sawanih-nigar, (3) the khafia-navis,—all three of whom sent written reports,— and (4) the harkarah, literally meaning a courier but really a spy, who brought oral news, though we have a few mentions of letters having been received from the last-named.

The terms waqai-navis (sometimes written as waqai-nigar also) and sawanih-nigar mean the same thing, viz., a writer or surveyor of occurrences. The only difference that I can suggest between them is that the waqai-navis was the more regular and public reporter of the two, while the sawanih-nigar was of the nature of a special commissioner or reporter on important cases only. But this explanation does not agree well with the Persian MS. that I have named the Manual of Officers' Duties. This much, however, is known that there was a waqai-navis attached to every field-army, province, and large town and a sawanih-nigar at special places and times only. The latter was most probably a spy and check on the former!

The waqai-navis attended when provincial viceroy held public court and he corded the occurrences then and there. The contents of the newsletter drafted by this reporter were communicated to the subahdar in the case of a field-army, to the generally command, before being despatched to the emperor. Whether the sawanih-nigar did the same thing, we do not know.

In the Manual, the waqai-navis is charged to send his reports of occurrences once every week and the sawanih-nigar eight times in a month. The language implies that the latter officer reported on the whole subah, while the former reported about a particular locality only, but this view is not tenable.

In the case of many of the provinces and all the minor armies, the posts of bakhshi and waqai-navis were combined in the same person.

The khufia-navis or 'secret writer', was a most confidential agent. He reported secretly on events without any communication with the local authorities, who often did not even know his name. All people were in mortal dread of these secret intelligencers and their office is, I understand, still maintained in some of our feudatory States.*

---

* The secret intelligencer is now called parcha-wala, which title must not be confounded with the parcha-navis described in the Manual, p. 53.

The newsletters (and in the case of the harkarahs the oral communications), were sent to an officer of the Court named the Darogha of Dak Chauki, i.e., Superintendent of Posts and Intelligence, who handed them unopened to the wazir for submission to the emperor. These four classes of public intelligencers acted under the orders of this Darogha, who was their official superior and protector. Sometimes an irate governor would publicly insult or beat the local news-writer for a report against himself, and then the Darogha would take up the cause of his subordinate and get the offending governor punished. The head of the Intelligence Department enjoyed great influence and trust in the reign of Aurangzib, who used to regard the spies as his eyes and ears. Amusing examples of it are given in

Hamiduddin's Ahkam-i-Alamgiri, translated into English by me as Anecdotes of Aurangzib. (See §§61, 62, 64 and 65.)

A newly-appointed waqai-navis is given the following shrewd advice in the Manual, pages 49—53: --

"Report the truth, lest the emperor should learn the facts from another source and punish you! Your work is delicate both sides have to be served. Deep sagacity and consideration should be employed so that 'both the Shaikh and the Book may remain in their proper places!' In the wards of most of the high officers, forbidden things are done. If you report them truly, the officers will be disgraced. If you do not, you yourself will be undone. Therefore, you should tell the lord of the ward, 'In your ward forbidden things are taking place; stop them.' If he gives a rude reply, you should threaten the kotwal of the ward by pointing out the misdeed. The lord of the ward will then know of it. Although the evil has not yet been removed from the ward, yet, if anyone reports the matter to the emperor, you can easily defend yourself by saying that you have informed the master of the ward and instructed the kotwal.

"In every matter write the truth; but avoid offending the nobles! Write after carefully verifying your statements.

"Waqai should be sent once a week, sawanih twice, and the akhbar of harkarahs once [? a month] and the despatches in cylinders (nalo) from the nazim and the diwan twice every month, in addition to urgent matters (which were to be reported immediately.)"

CHAPTER V

Taxation of Land.

§ 1. Chronic antagonism of the Indian peasant to the revenue collector.

A careful student of Indian history is very much struck by the chronic antagonism between the rent-payer and the rent-receiver from very ancient times. European travellers in India have noticed how the ryot was averse to pay even his legitimate rent and that force had to be employed to get from him the dues of the State. [Storia do Mogor, ii. 450.] On the other hand, in Sanskrit literature as well as Persian Courtannals we read how the "King's men"—i.e., revenue officials and Court underlings, —preyed on the peasantry and in both ages the sovereign is called upon to save the ryots from such bloodsuckers.

The Indian peasant's habitual reluctance to pay revenue was partly due to the fact that he derived little benefit from the Government in return for the revenue; but it was mainly because of the uncertainty of that Government. I have explained already how the State in Mughal India performed no socialistic duties, but simply undertook to defend the country from invaders and rebels. Even this work of national defence was badly done at times, while the policing of the villages against thieves and robbers was done by a village agency which was not remunerated out of the revenue. Thus, the ryot received nothing visible in return for which Government might fairly demand from him a share of the fruits of his labour.

Secondly, changes of dynasty were so frequent, wars of succession within the same dynasty so much the rule rather than the exception and the invasion of neighbouring countries (in Sanskrit digvijay, in Persian giri,) was so universally regarded as a duty by Hindu Rajahs and Muslim Sultans alike, that the peasant in India seldom knew for certain to whom to pay the revenue, even when he was willing to pay it. He naturally wanted to avoid having to pay the same money twice over. It was (he felt) wiser to wait for some months or years, even at the risk of some beating in the meantime, and see which side became firmly planted on the throne and then pay the revenue to it. But the arrear of revenue which thus accumulated could never be paid in full after such long delays because much of the peasant's stock was eaten up by him and much of it plundered during the unsettled state of the country.

Many centuries of political insecurity and revolution have left in the mind of the Indian peasant even of the 20th century, a subconscious but ingrained belief that wars of succession are quite in the nature of things and that whenever the Government is engaged in a war anywhere, a wise peasant ought to think twice before paying the revenue due.

During the late war with Germany, several khas-mahal ryots in Chittagong hesitated to pay their land-tax and told the Deputy Collector, "If the Kohisur comes will he not ask for our revenue over again? Save us, Sir, from the double payment."

I was in a North Bengal village at the time of the death of King Edward VII. The first question which the local ryots asked me on hearing of His present Majesty's succession[iii] was, "Are not his kinsmen disputing his accession to the throne?" We can easily imagine the long ages of disorder and oppression that lie behind this traditional belief among our villagers.

§2. The peasant ever in arrears of payment.

Hence, the collection of the revenue was always the result of a struggle between the ryot and the sarkar, and the arrears were seldom if ever cleared. The next logical step in this vicious circle was for the Government collectors to exact from the ryot, under the name of the never-to-be-extinguished arrears, everything except his bare subsistence. In most parts of Mughal India the ryot was, therefore, like the French peasantry in the reign of Louis XV trying to escape the unjust taille or the cottier peasantry of Ireland who were ever in debt to their landlords.

There was this difference, however, that in ore-British times there was no eviction for default, no starvation of the peasantry (except when there was a local famine, with no communication writhe more fruitful parts of the country.) In the fiarly and mediaeval times, the peasant was left in his holding and left with enough to feed him (except when the entire harvest failed.) The old custom of payment by the division of the crop (the batai system) was an advantage to him, as the payment depended on the actual harvest of the year, unlike the modern money-rent which is an amount fixed irrespective of the yield of different years. In those days of constant war and disorder, the peasant was also cherished and valued because his landlord had need for him as an armed retainer. Indeed, competition for tenants among the zamindars was the rule and the poorer peasants sometimes escaped from one zamindari to another in the hope of getting rid of their arrears with the former and of faring better under a new landlord. Cases of such fugitive ryots were very frequent in North Bengal only forty years ago.

§3. Illegal imposts on peasants, condemned hy the Government Head.

The natural tendency of the ryot to withhold or refuse the payment of revenue and the failure of the State to give him a clean slate every three or five years by writing off his arrears, were the chief causes of trouble in the Mughal revenue department. The evil was agggregated by the greed of the revenue underlings and of some of the emperors even. When I discuss the list of abwahs or unauthorised exactions from the people in Mughal times, you will perceive the wonderful fertility of the human invention in devising means for squeezing money out of the people, —at birth, throughout life and even after death. All these ahwahs were not directly paid by the peasant; several of them affected the smaller dealers and townspeople too. But as our population is predominently agricultural and most of the articles for sale came from the land, the weight of the abwabs pressed most heavily on the ryots.

It is only fair to add that in respect of the abwabs, there was a clear conflict of policy between the better sort of Emperors on the one hand and the revenue collectors on the other. These Emperors are for ever issuing orders to their officers to show leniency and consideration to the peasants in collecting the revenue, to give up all abwabs, and to relieve local distress; and the revenue officers are as often squeezing everything out of the peasants except the barest subsistence. A solemn proclamation is issued by one Emperor abolishing all ahwabs and urging all his officials, "at present and in future" to obey these instructions. But these very ahwabs crop up again and have to be abolished by his succeed with another proclamation, which has exactly the same efficacy as the first. English readers will find painful illustrations of it in Thomas's Revenue Resources of the Mughal Empire published in 1871, which may be supplemented by my translation of Aurangzib's Revenue Regulations published in the J.A.S.B. in 1906*, and the list of abwabs abolished by Aurangzib in 1673, as given in this lecture.

* Reprinted in my Studies in Mughal India 169—197.

The policy of the supreme head of the Mughal Government not to commit any exaction on the ryot is manifest from the contemporary histories and letters and can be proved to have been a reality and not merely a pious wish. Several instcinces are recorded in the reigns of Shah Jahan and Aurangzib in which harsh and exacting revenue collectors and even provincial viceroys were dismissed on the complaints of their subjects reaching the emperor's ears. A characteristic anecdote to the same effect is told in India Office Library Persian Manuscript No. 370, interleaf facing folio 68. It clearly illustrates Shah Jahan's eagerness to do justice and even liberality to the peasantry, and I shall narrate it here.

"One day," so runs the story, "Shah Jahan was looking through the revenue returns of his empire and discovered that in a certain village the revenue for the present year was entered as higher by a few thousands [dam?] than that of past years. Immediately he ordered the High Diwan Sadullah Khan to be brought to the Presence for explaining the difference. Sadullah Khan was then sitting in his treasury with an open bundle of revenue papers before him and his eyes dozing in consequence of his daily and nightly attention to the business of his department. The royal messengers brought him to the emperor in exactly the same condition [and dress.] Shah jahan asked him for the cause of the increase in the assessment. After a local inquiry it was found out that the river had receded a little and a new tract of land had risen above water-level, causing cin addition to the area of the village and the income of the State. On the Emperor asking whether the land in question was khalsa or aima, a further inquiry was made, and it was found to adjoin a piece of rent-free grant of land (aima.) Then Shah Jahan cried out in wrath, 'The water over that tract of land has dried in response to the lamentations of the orphans, widows and poor [of the place]; it is a divine gift to them, and you have dared to appropriate it to the State! If a desire to spare God's creation had not restrained me, I should have ordered the execution of that second Satan, the oppressive faujdar [who has collected revenue from this new land.] It will be enough punishment to dismiss him as a warning to others to refrain from such wicked acts of injustice. Order the excess collection to be immediately refunded to the peasants entitled to it.'

This anecdote may or may not have been true in every letter, but it shows the atmosphere and the public belief in Shah jahan's kindness to his subjects.

§4. Lower revenue officials were harsh and extortionate.

The lower officials of Mughal India were incurably corrupt, while the highest were, on the whole, just and statesman-like, except an occasional diwan who inflated the revenue demand on paper and farmed the collection to the highest bidder with ruinous consequences, as can be illustrated from the revenue history of Orissa in the 17th century.

The subahdar of Orissa wrote in 1662, "The mahals of Crownland have been reduced to desolation and their affairs have fallen into confusion in consequence of the harsh assessment of an unreasonable amount of revenue and the neglect of details by the [new] diwan, Muhammad Hashim. He transacts business in this way: when a candidate for krori-ship accepts the post, Hashim imposes on him the paper assessment of the parganah and sends him there, before he can learn about the [actual] yield of the place. After a short time, another man is secured for the post and Hashim Khan taking money for himself from this man, dismisses the former krori, appoints the second man and makes him promise a larger revenue than the first collector had engaged for. After a little time, a third man appears, offering a still higher sum to the State and he is sent as collector to the parganah!...The Khan has thus increased the revenue [on paper] twofold in some places and threefold in others, while the ryots, unable to pay, have fled away and the villages have turned into a wilderness." [Studies in Mughal India, 223—224.]

The man was shortly afterwards removed from office.

The Emperor, the High Diwan and even the subahdar may have been just and kind in their treatment of the peasantry. But the lower official or revenue underling was the man on the spot, the person in direct relations with the ryots and therefore his harshness and greed affected the ryots far more effectively than the far-off Emperor's or Chancellor's kind intentions and benevolent proclamations. This fact was well-known in the 17th century.

The great and good Diwan-i-ala, Sadullah Khan, used to remark that a diwan who did not do justice to the ryots was a demon sitting with a pen and inkpot before him. The propriety of this epigram will become clear when I tell you that in the Persian alphabet "a" is a long vertical line with a sharp downward point like an Indian reed-pen, while the letter "n" is formed by a circle open at the top, just like an indigenous inkpot. The word "diw" means 'an evil spirit;' and hence diwan can be analysed into "diw" followed by "a" or a pen and "n" or an inkpot! (Ruqaat-i-Alamgiri, letter No. 154.)

In fact, the cunning of the local officials and the subordinates of the revenue department was too much even for the lord of the Peacock Throne, and we find more than 50 abwabs flourishing immediately after the death of this very Shah Jahan.

§5. Why revenue officials exacted perquisites.

The exaction of perquisites and presents by the officials from the subahdar downwards was one of the greatest evils of mediaeval administrations, in the East and the West alike. In the Mughal Empire the evil was aggravated by three other causes, viz., (1) the custom of offering presents to the emperor and the princes by the higher officers and to the higher officers by the lower, (2) the nominal salaries paid to the lower officers and (3) the submissive, indifferent spirit of the people.

Immemorial custom and the prevalent notions of social etiquette, as well as the more worldly motive of keeping one's superiors in good humour, made it imperative for the subadidars to offer rare or valuable presents to the emperor on his birthday and also at their visits to the Court. The High Chancellor also had to be propitiated by similar means.

This pressure passed from the top to the bottom, though it was unintentional, and its real effects were not fully realised by the head of the State. The emperors, without meaning it, squeezed the subahdars and the subahdars did so to the zamindars; the provincial diwan had to gratify the High Diwan and therefore he had to squeeze the subordinate collectors of the revenue and these men at the bottom of the official ladder squeezed the ryots.

This was quite distinct from giving bribes to cause a failure of justice or to win a favour that was undeserved by the man or injurious to the real interests of the State. Taking bribes was recognised as a wicked and disgraceful thing even in Mughal times, though it was extensively practised under the veil of secrecy.

The low salaries paid by the Government had necessarily to be supplemented by the clerks and other subordinates exacting unauthorised fees from the men who had to do business with them. It was called "the writer's fee" haqq-ut-taharir (or tahariri as used in the law-courts and some other offices here even now.) In the Manual, (p. 72) the auditor (mushrif) is advised, "Take the writer's fee that the people pay you willingly, for how else can a man deserving Rs. 50 but paid a salary of Rs. 20 a month, contrive to live?"

§6. The krori or collector of revenue of a district.

The actual revenue collector was the krori, so styled because he was placed in charge of a tract theoretically expected to yield a revenue of one kror of dam, i.e., 2½ lakhs of Rupees. The arrangement was Akbar's (Ain, i. 13.) But the title of krori was continued in later times irrespective of the amount of revenue to be collected by this officer. It latterly meant simply 'a collector of State dues', and we have a class of kroris of ganj, i.e., collectors of markets.

"The krori ought to entertain a body of militia (sehbandi) proportionate to his jurisdiction and collect the revenue without negligence and at the right time. He should not demand mahsul (the State due in cash or kind) from places not yet capable of paying, lest their ryots should run away. He should urge his subordinates not to realise anything in excess of the regulations, lest he should, in the end, be subjected to wasilat (examination of accounts with a view to detect peculation.) He should be honest." (Manual, p. 64.)

The duties and necessary virtues of an ideal "collector of the revenue" under Akbar are described in the Ain, ii. 43—47; but he seems to have been a higher officer than a krori of the 17th century.

The sanad appointing a new krori runs thus: "Collect the revenue season by season, as assessed by the amin and pay it to the fotahdar. With the advice of the faujdar and amin, carefully deposit the [accumulated] money in the imperial treasury, giving a receipt for it to the fotahdar. Send to the Government Record Office your abstract accounts and statements of income and disbursement and other papers, as laid down in the regulations. Do not collect any abwab, such as nahib (?), the collector's perquisite (tahsildari) &c., lest the money should be taken back from the offender, and he be dismissed."

§7- The amin and the qanungo.

Amin literally means an umpire or arbitrator, a trustee for others. The essence of his office was to be an impartial umpire between the State demanding revenue and the individual ryots paying it.

The Manual of the Duties of Officers (61— 63) gives us the following information about the amin and his work: —

"The amin should know the regulations (zabita) well and be an honest and expert man, well-versed in the quality (good or bad) of every affair. He should make the assessment (mushakhas) according to the rules and let no steal Government money.

"The amin's work is to cause the kingdom to be cultivated. Before the commencement of the season of cultivation, he should take from the qanungoes the preceding ten years' papers of the revenue assessment and area of the villages, ride to the villages in company with the kroris, chaudhuris, qanungoes and zamindars, inquire into the conditions of the villages, as regards their [culturable] area and the actual number of ploughs, compare the area given in the papers of the qanungo with the real area and if the two do not agree call upon the qanungo to explain the excess (in the case of excess) and censure the headmen (in the case of shortage), saying "Why did the qanungo give a false return and why did the headman tell lies?"

Then inquire whether the existing ploughs are sufficient for the cultivators of the village. If not, then grant taqavi (agricultural loans), proportioned to the area of the culturable soil of the village, for the purchase of oxen and seeds, taking bonds* from the headmen for the recovery of the loan with the first instalment of the [next] year and indemnity-bonds (muchilka) from the kroris that they would realise the loan with the first instalment of the [next] year."

---

* These bonds (tamassuk) were to be endorsed by the chaudhuri as security, sealed by the qazi and attested by the qanungo and zamindar.

The sanad appointing an amin runs thus:

"Do your work with honesty and truthfulness. Exert yourself to perpetuate the cultivation and increase the habitation. You will be held responsible for the portion of the collected revenue deposited with the fotahdar which he keeps in his hands in arrear (i.e., without paying it into the treasury.) Urge the krori to collect the revenue according to his own assessment and deposit it with the fotahdar. Give temporary receipts (chitha) for the money that the ryots pay to the fotahdar, under your seal and the fotahdar's signature and at the time of payment of revenue in full (bebaqi) make up the account according to this chitha. Do not collect any abwab like bald dasti and tahsildari, as all these have been forbidden by the emperor. Warn the chaudhuris and qanungoes not to exact any such cess."

The papers which the amin and the krori had to submit to the Diwan's office are enumerated in "Z. 34a and D. 89a" and those that they had to keep, in Z.6 a & b.

The QANUNGO, as the name implies, was a walking dictionary of the prevailing rules and practices (qanun), and a storehouse of information as to procedure, precedents, land-history of the past, &c. The Ain (ii. 66) styles him "the refuge of the husbandman" [See also Ain, ii, 47 n.]

They were "village revenue-officers who recorded all circumstances within their sphere which concerned landed property and the realisation of the revenue, keeping registers of the value, tenure, extent, and transfers of lands, assisting in the measurement and survey of the lands, reporting deaths and successions of revenue-payers and explaining, when required, local practices and public regulations; they were paid by rent-free lands and various allowances and perquisites." (Wilson, 260.)

The Manual (34—35) instructs a new qanungo thus: "The Emperor's business goes on in reliance on your papers. To your office belong the papers of division (taqsim), comparison (muazana) &c.....Keep two copies of the records, —one in your house and the other in your office (in charge of your gumashta) so that one at least may be saved in case of fire or flood."

§8. Abwabs or illegal cesses

I shall now discuss in detail the abwahs or exactions made on various pretexts in addition to the regular land-revenue or custom-duty. These imposts were again and again declared by the Muhammadan sovereigns to be illegal and forbidden within their realms, but they soon reappeared with some changes in their items. Thomas in his *Revenue Resources of the Mughal Empire* has given from Persian lists of the ahwahs abolished by Firuz Shah Tughlaq (1375 A.D.) and Akbar (about 1590.) Those prohibited by Aurangzib in a farman dated 29th April 1673, are enumerated in Mirat-i-Ahmadi pp. 303—304, Z, f. 135 and D. f. 102. But these three sources do not agree in all points; Mirat names forty-one, Z. seventy-four and D. seventy-eight ahwabs as abolished at this time. In Bengal nineteen such imposts continued to be levied but from the tenants only, till the 19th century, when the British law-courts finally put an end to them as illegal. (Rampini's Bengal Tenancy Act, 4th ed., pp. 255—256.) We are thus in a position to make a comparative study of the growth of ahwahs through several centuries of our history.

The ahwahs naturally fall into six broad classes: —

a) Duties on the local sale of produce, like the municipal octroi duty of certain towns in modern India but taken by the State.
b) Fee on the sale of immovable property.
c) Perquisites exacted by the officials for their own benefit and fees or commissions levied on behalf of the State, on almost every conceivable occasion.
d) License-tax for plying certain trades.
e) Forced subscriptions.
f) Special imposts on the Hindus. Aurangzib's abolitions are given below.

A. Duties on the sale of produce: —

1. Fish.

2. Oil or ghee. [Both Z and D. read a karuah, which I read as raughan-i-karuah or mustard seed oil.]

3. Chungi on opium. [Reading doubtful.]

4. Cowdung cakes,

5. Milk and curds.

6. Dhak leaves and bark of the babul (gum) from the jungles. [All three sources differ in reading. Babul in Mirat only.]

7. Kitchen vegetables.

8. Grass, fuel wood and brambles from the jungles.

9. Ground-rent for stalls in bazaars. [All three read hasil-i-tah (or batta)-i-bazari. The ground-rent for stalls in bazars, called the pandari tax, was abolished by Aurangzib in certain towns in 1659. See History of Aurangzib, iii. 89—90.]

10. Tobacco tax. [Abolished in 1666, under circumstances described by Manucci, ii. 175. See History of Aurangzib, iii. 91.]

11. Roses for rose-water. [Doubtful reading.]

12. Earthen pots and dishes made in the villages and towns.

B. Fee on the sale of property: —

13. On the sale or mortgage of land.

14. On the sale of houses (haveli.)

15. On the sale of captives (barda faroshi,)

C. Perquisites of officials and fees or commissions of the State: —

16. Rahdari or remuneration of road patrols. [Abolished by Aurangzib in 1659. The hardships and abuses connected with this tax are fully described in my History of Aurangzib, iii. 88—89 and *Studies in Mughal India, pp. 162—163*. In the Crownlands alone this tax used to yield 25 lakhs of Rupees a year at the time of its abolition.]

17. Tax (hasil) on the hire of carts, camels, and messengers.

18. Tax on stone weights, ["at the time of stamping with the official stamp the stoneweights, iron weights etc., "—added by Mirat.]

19. Fee for census of head-dresses, heads, and houses (dastar-shumari, sar-shumari, khanah-shumari.) We know that houses were counted to complete village records in Akbar's reign, but we have no mention in the Persian histories or the accounts of the European travellers of any census of the population being taken in Mughal India.

20. One-fourth of the amount in dispute in money-suits belonged to the State (like the court-fee of our times.) Aurangzib abolished this exaction as well as the payment of the fines and thanks-offerings which had the sanction of ancient usage and even of Muslim judicial practice.

21. Shash dami [a fee of three-twentieth of a Rupee. Not clear.]

22. The customary perquisite (muqarrari) taken from men in receipt of rent-free grants of land (madad-i-ma'sh)

23. The exaction of presents in kind from such men at the time of marking out their plots of land (chak bandi.)

24. Fee for the appraising (muqimi) of land. [Mirat reads, "muqimi for the sale of houses acquired by Government."]

25. Tax on the grass of pastures.

26. Tax on the birth of male children.

27. Fee of the darogha and the kotwali [Mirat adds "for setting up the weighing balance," dandi.]

28. Fee for watching over pack-oxen, camel-litters, dolis (litters carried on men's shoulders) chests and packages [? in marketplaces. Evidently collected for the benefit of the police.]

29. Ancient perquisites on speciel occasions and with special names, — saliana (once in a year), fasalana (once in a season), mahiana (once in a month), rozana (daily), on the 'Ids, dastar-'barari (?), etc.

30. Ferry tax collected on rivers that have dried up [and can be crossed on foot]!

31. Price of paper [used in the official records and receipts to the peasants.]

32. A tax on every iron cauldron in which molasses are boiled, [Mirat adds, "But the duty on the liquid sugar is to be levied as laid down in the regulations."]

33. Presents (peshkash) taken by newly arrived officials from grain-dealers and others, and in some places from the banjaras.

34. Governors must not billet themselves in private houses, mosques, or shops without the consent of their owners.

35. Reward (rukhsatana) taken for carrying letters from the [imperial] camp &c.

36. The guards at the gates of forts must not take anything from the people passing through them.

37. Mahsul-i-sar-wa-basti. [?Sar-basti means 'exemption from payment, not entitled to taxation'.]

D. License-tax on trades: —

38. From butchers.

39. From footmen (piddas.)

40 & 41. From cotton-dressers and sugar-cane-pressers, going to a new place to start business there.

42. From thatchers (of roofs) and watchmen (pasban.)

43. From printers of (cotton) cloth, at the time of stamping them.

44. Headman's dues (muqaddami) on the hire of camels.

45. From brick-makers.

46. From mummers, who used to put on disguises and go to houses where marriages were being celebrated, to entertain the people. [A letter of Aurangzib suggests that such mummings were altogether put down in Kashmir late in his reign.]

47. From brokers (dalal.) [Text obscure.]

48. Tax on matchlocks [? or from gunsmiths. D. only source.]

As Shihabuddin Talish complained (in 1666), "From the first occupation of India and its ports by the Muslims to the end of Shah jahan's reign, it was a rule and practice to exact hasil from every trader, —from the rose-vendor to the clay-vendor, from the weaver of fine linen to that of coarse cloth."

E. Forced subscriptions and gifts: —

49. Forced labour and [compulsory lighting of] lamps on the 'Id festival.

50 The [compulsory] lighting of lamps in the nights of shah-i-barat, diwali, the first ten days of the month of Shawwal, &c.

51. Bhet and begdra. [Reading doubtful. D. and Z. give bhet banjara and bhet kara respectively. Mirat reads "bhet banjara-harasum i dandiha az chungi wa ghaira and gives immediately afterwards No. 27 above. One of the abwabs abolished in Bengal was called 'bhet and hegar' or presents and gratuitous labour. See Rampini, loc. cit.]

52. Order for fruits &c. [for the emperor's table, issued on the provinces and supplied gratis.] [This is the reading of Z. and D. Mirat, however, reads "(compensation) for injury to fruits &c. ordered" and a few lines later adds "The fruits of (i.e., intended to be sent to the Emperor by) relays of horsemen, are misappropriated or damaged by the traffic of the men of the villages on the roads near them and [the State carriers] therefore trouble the wayfarers." We know that mangoes used to be sent to the emperor regularly from Allahabad, Malwa and Khandesh, pomegranates from Jodhpur and Tatta, and several other fruits from Gujrat.]

F. Imposts on the Hindus: —

53. Tax on bathing in the Ganges and other (holy) rivers.

54. Tax on the carrying of the bones of dead Hindus for being thrown into the Ganges. Several other prohibitions of Aurangzib given by our authorities in this connection, do not refer to illegal cesses remitted but to practices contrary to the Quran which he prohibited. These have nothing to do with taxation and therefore cannot be dealt with here.

Several of the items above are given with great diffidence, as the Persian texts are very obscure and corrupt. I shall, therefore, enumerate here the cesses which were forbidden by the Calcutta High Court as their special names are correctly known:

(a) Zabita hatta or customary levy,

(b) mihmani or guest money and nazrana or presents, (c) bardana, batta and kotwali tobacco,

(d) chanda or subscription,

(e) qazi's fees,

(f) najai or tax assessed upon the cultivators present to make up for any deficiency arising from the death or disappearance of their neighbours

(g) a cess of so much gur or molasses on every maund manufactured

(h) a cess for grazing cattle on a jotedar's own jote but within the zamindar's estate,

(i) rakhumat or miscellaneous items,

(j) parabi or festival cess,

(k) patwari's fee,

(l) patwaris wages, sidha or daily rations,

(m) pasbani or watchman's wages,

(n) bhet and begar, &c.

CHAPTER VI

MUGHAL RULE: ITS ACHIEVEMENTS AND FAILURE.

§1. Political effects of Mughal Government.

What is the legacy of Mughal rule to India? The Mughal empire at its greatest extent covered a larger portion of our country than the Indian dominions of Asoka or Samudragupta. These Hindu empires also consisted of loosely united collections of independent provinces which did not acquire any homogeneity, nor create a sense of political unity or nationality among their people. Each province led its own life, continued its old familiar system of government (though under the agents of the central power), and used its local tongue. On the other hand, the two hundred years of Mughal rule, from the accession of Akbar to the death of Muhammad Shah (1556—1749), gave to the whole of Northern India and much of the Deccan also, oneness of the official language, administrative system, and coinage and also a popular lingua franca for all classes except the Hindu priests and the stationary village folk. Even outside the territory directly administered by the Mughal Emperors, their administrative system, official nomenclature, court etiquette and monetary type were borrowed, more or less, by the neighbouring Hindu Rajahs.

All the twenty Indian subahs of the Mughal empire were governed by means of exactly the same administrative machinery, with exactly the same procedure and official titles. Persian was the one language used in all office records, farmans, sanads, land-grants, passes, despatches and receipts. The same monetary standard prevailed throughout the empire, with coins having the same names, the same purity, and the same denominations and differing only in the name of the mint-town. Officials and soldiers were frequently transferred from one province to another. Thus, the native of one province felt himself almost at home in another province; traders and travellers passed most easily from city to city, suhah to subah, and all realised the imperial oneness of this vast country. Nationality, however, could not result from this political union because the people had no civil liberty, no share in the government of their country. They were not citizens but merely equal subjects of one empire.

The second gift of the Muslims to India is historical literature. The chronological sense was very imperfectly developed among the Hindus, probably because being a race of Vedantists they kept their gaze fixed on eternity and despised this fleeting world and its ephemeral occurrences. The Hindus in the pre-Muhammadan days composed no true history at all; only four political biographies have been preserved in Sanskrit and in all of them the facts lie buried under a mass of flowers of rhetoric, tricks of style and round-about expressions. In none of them have we dates. Even when the Hindus learnt Persian and wrote histories or memoirs of their times in that language in imitation of Persian models, their works were wofully lacking in dates.

On the other hand, the Arab intellect is dry, methodical and matter of fact, like that of the Jews, Phoenicians, and other Semitic races. All their records contain a chronological framework, and their letters almost always give the day and month of writing. Whatever the historical literature of the Muhammadans may miss out, they never fail to give a wealth of dates. We thus get a solid basis for our historical study. The use of one era, viz., that dating from the Prophet's flight and calculated according to the lunar year, was a great advantage to the Muslims, as it gave to the entire world under Muhammadan sway a common system for dating events,—which affords a striking contrast to the bewildering variety of eras, length of months and length of the year that we find in Hindu inscriptions and books. To take one example only, the Hindu luni-solar year, in which each month is divided into the dark and bright fortnights (badi and sudi), was not the same in Northern India and Southern as regards the day of commencement and the intercalary month. Hence it is next to impossible to convert such dates in the old Marathi records of the 17th century into the Christian era with any chance of correctness. The Muslim dates follow one uniform *and well-known system.

---

*There was often the difference of one day as between India and other countries at the commencement of certain months, owing to the difference in the visibility of the new moon in the two places.

§2. Contact with the outer world.

Thirdly, the Mughal empire and even its so-called Pathan predecessor, re-established the contact between India and the outer Asiatic world, which had been destroyed with the decline of Buddhism in its home. Through the passes of the Afghan frontier the stream of population and trade flowed peacefully into India from Bukhara pnd Samarqand, Balkh and Khurasan, Khwarizm and Persia because Afghanistan belonged to the ruler of Delhi, till near the end of the Mughal empire. Through the Bolan pass leading from India to Qandahar in South Afghanistan and thence to Persia, as many as 14,000 camel-loads of merchandise passed every year in the reign of Jahangir, early in the 17th century. The ports on our western coast—Tatta, Broach, Surat, Chaul, Rajapur, Goa (before its annexation by the Portuguese) and Karwar, —were so many doors between India and the outer world that could be reached by sea, such as Arabia, Persia, Turkey, Egypt, Barbery, Abyssinia and even Zanzibar. From the eastern port of Masulipatam, belonging to the Sultans of Golkonda up to 1687 and thereafter to the Mughals, —ships used to sail for Ceylon, Sumatra, Java, Siam and even China. The Arabs are born traders —like their cousins the Jews, —and they take kindly to a sea-faring life. The trade of the west coast of India had been their monopoly in the 1st century of the Christian era (as we learn from the Periplus of the Erythrean Sea,) And now the conversion of the entire Near East and Middle East with parts of the Malay world to their faith and their sacred tongue gave them the greatest advantage in the sea-borne trade of Asia and Africa.

What the Muhammadans began the English have completed. Today India's isolation is broken, and she has been switched on to the currents—economic, cultural, and political, —of the entire outer world.

§3. Religious changes in India due to Islam.

Fourthly, Hunter and some other European writers have held that the monotheistic or at least anti-Brahman and anti-caste movements among the Hindus in the Middle Ages were due to the Influence of Islam. But we have to bear in mind that all the higher thinkers, all the religious reformers, all the devout bhaktas among the Hindus from the remotest time have proclaimed the principle of monotheism and recognised the one supreme God behind the countless deities of popular worship.

Therefore, it is not historically true that Islam taught the Hindus monotheism. What really happened was that these dissenting movements among the Hindus of mediaeval India received a great impetus from the presence of the Muhammadans in our immediate neighbourhood.

Many sects arose which tried to harmonise Islam and Hinduism and to afford a common meeting-ground to the devout men of both creeds, without emphasising their differences of ritual, dogma, and other external marks of faith. This was the aim of Kabir and Dadu, Nanak and Chaitanya. They made converts freely from Hindus and Muslims and rejected the rigid orthodoxy of the Brahman and the Mulla alike.

So, too, the Sufi movement afforded a common platform to the more learned and devout minds among the Hindus and Muhammadans. Unlike the above-mentioned popular religions of mediaeval India, Sufism never extended to the illiterate people. It was essentially a faith often an intellectual-emotional enjoyment — reserved for the philosophers, authors, and mystics free from bigotry. The eastern variety of Sufism is mainly an off shoot of the Vedanta of the Hindus, and it rapidly spread and developed in India from the time of Akbar onwards.

A huge mass of Sufi literature in Persian was produced by the Hindus. Though of the poorest literary quality, it shows the wide prevalence of this faith among our people, especially in the 17th and 18th centuries, probably as a refuge from the political disorder and economic decay attending the decline of the Mughal empire. These popular religions and Sufi philosophy tended to bring the ruling race and the dominated people closer together.

§4. Muslim influence on society, architecture, and arts.

Fifthly, many elements of modern Hindu social manners in Northern India are due to Islamic influence, which also modified the dress of our gentry and popular literature to some extent. The masses, however, remained unaffected by it.

Next, hunting, hawking and many games became Muhammadanised in method and terminology. Persian, Arabic and Turkish words have entered largely into the Hindi Bengali and even Marathi languages. An exact parallel is afforded by the influence of the Norman Conquest upon English life and language.

The art of war was very highly developed by the Muslims, partly by borrowing from Europe through Turkey—and, to a lesser extent, through Persia. The rajahs of the Hindu period used to lead petty forces or the confederation of a number of distinct petty contingents. But the Mughal Emperors commanded vast armies obeying one supreme voice, the handling of which required greater organising power and capacity, and thus gave greater opportunities for the display of generalship than was possible in the Hindu period. From the point of view of mere organisation (as distinct from real efficiency as an instrument of war), the Mughal army was almost perfect in every branch.

The system of fortification was greatly improved by the Muhammadans in India, as a natural consequence of the general advance of civilisation and the introduction of artillery.

Muhammadan rule caused a distinct advance in architecture. The Hindu kings lavished their wealth and skill on temples; their palaces have all perished and seem to have been of no high or costly pattern. But the Muhammadans built palaces and tombs in addition to mosques. The semi-circular radiating arch and the vaulted dome are peculiarly Muhammadan and so also are geometrically laid out gardens.

In the domain of the fine arts the richest contribution of the Muhammadans is the Indo-Saracen school of painting. The Mughals introduced Chinese painting by way of Bukhara and Khurasan, and at the Court of Akbar this art mingled with the indigenous Hindu painting, of which traditions still lingered amidst neglect and poverty. The result of the fusion was that the Chinese characteristics were rapidly dropped, and a purely Indian appearance was given to pieces marked by undeniable foreign technique. (Studies in Mughal India, 290-291.) Thus, in painting there was a true revival, and the highest genius was displayed by our artists in this field in the Mughal age. This style holds the field even now under the name of "Indian art" or "Mughal painting." The so-called Rajput school is only the Mughal or Indo-Saracen style with Hindu mythological or epic subjects.

We have seen that Muslim rule in general and the Mughal empire in particular, achieved many things great and good for mediaeval India. Why then did it fail? In order to answer this question, it is necessary for us to examine the strength and weakness of the Muslim State in India.

§5. Elements of strength in the Muslim position in India.

The Muhammadans in India at first possessed the advantage of a common language, common traditions, a common religion, common teachers, and a common political status in the midst of a conquered and alien population. The absence of caste distinctions and the democratic spirit of Islam fused the conquering sect into a brotherhood. Hence, the State in Muslim India, before its degeneration in the 18th century, often displayed an unexampled solidarity in the face of foreign invasion. Another source of the strength of the Muslim rulers of India was that they wisely retained the old system of village administration and method of revenue collection of the Hindu times unchanged, and even employed Hindu officials almost exclusively in the revenue department. The result was that the lives of the millions of our villagers were undisturbed by the dynastic changes at the capital and they had no reason to be discontented with their new masters and to rise against them.

§6. Muhammadan settlers Indianised.

But the long stay of the invading Muslim races in India gradually destroyed their alien character and gave to them a purely Indian stamp, till at last from the 17th century onwards it became increasingly difficult for the Indian Muhammadans to absorb readily into their society newcomers from Bukhara Persia or Arabia. (This was a change quite distinct from the deterioration in their physique and colour under the Indian climate.) The Indo-Muhammadans adopted many Indian customs beliefs, articles of food (esp. betel-leaf) and dress and even an Indian language, namely Hindustani (zaban-i-Hindavi, 'the Indian tongue*), which is Sanskritic in its grammatical structure though its vocabulary is full of Persian and Arabic words in addition to Hindi. Thus, in the course of centuries the Indo-Muhammadans almost completely drifted apart from their brethren of the outer Asiatic world. The later Muhammadan immigrants into India were absorbed in the local population but only after the lapse of two or three generations, by which time they had acquired the distinctive Indian character and given up their foreign peculiarities.

Centuries of residence in this country in the midst of a vastly more numerous Hindu elements and a purely Indian environment, gradually fused the Muhammadans in certain respects with the indigenous population. The Indo- Muhammadans largely married local women and admitted enormous numbers of converts from Hinduism (or corrupt Buddhism), with the result that they quickly lost their purity of blood and distinctive racial characteristics. They also adopted many Hindu customs beliefs and even ways of life. The popular religions of mediaeval India, Sufism, the Urdu language, and Indo-Saracen art were the common property of the conquerors and the conquered and tended to blend them together, as closely as the granite walls of the caste system would permit. Many Muhammadan saints (pirs) were worshipped by the lower classes of the Hindus, and renowned Muslim saints were adored by stout champions of Hindu orthodoxy like Shivaji. The ignorant Muhammadan peasantry of Bengal and even of other provinces where no vigilant reforming mulla was present, took part in Hindu religious festivals and the worship of popular villagegods, just as in Bihar low-class Hindus take part in the Muharram procession as enthusiastically as the Muhammadans.

Thus, while the old scriptures and strict theory kept the two sects apart, a common destiny and the common weal and woe of life under the same Indian sun drew them together, except for occasional crescentades by a puritan Sultan or Padishah.

§7. Disruptive forces in the State.

Muhammadan dominion over India was spread more by individual chieftains and adventurers than by the direct action of any organised central power. There was, no doubt, always a nominal Sultan as the theoretical king but the enthusiastic and fanatical generals who conquered the Hindu provinces beyond the frontiers, owed only a nominal allegiance to this central Government and they were usually masters of their own troops and treasures, instead of being merely salaried servants removable at a word from the Sultan. Macaulay in his famous essay on the Popes has described how the Roman Catholic Church utilises the enthusiasm of unattached or irregular fanatics to convert new peoples without having to devote its regular priesthood to the work but deriving full advantage from the voluntary action of these enthusiasts. Similar was the policy of the central monarch of Muslim India during the period of expansion and conquest. He maintained excellent relations with the enterprising adventurers of his own faith; he profited by their bold initiative and zealous exertions, without having to spend his own men or money. At the same time, he kept them pleased by not insisting upon too much subordination to himself or too rigid a control of the provinces won and ruled by them.

This arrangement worked well so long as there were fresh lands to conquer. But when the Muslim expansion reached its furthest possible limit eastward and southward, rebellion, intrigue, murder of sovereigns and chaotic wars of succession became frequent, because the old plan of Muslim conquest left as its legacy a centrifugal or disruptive spirit tending to local autonomy. These frequent changes of dynasty and violent civil wars hindered the growth of civilisation, the economic prosperity of the country, and the development of institutions. As the Latin proverb has it, "In the midst of arms, the laws are silent."

§8. Gradual decline of the people.

There was no hereditary peerage in Islam, I no recognition of the right of private property. Every nobleman's lands and personal effects were confiscated to the State on his death. If his sons got any portion of them, it was as a mere act of grace on the part of the sovereign. This rule, no doubt, prevented the slackening of effort but it also destroyed the basis of civilisation, viz., the accumulation of savings from the past for improvement in the future. All was ephemeral in such a society; the economic prosperity and position built up by an individual noble was levelled to the ground at his death and his son had to begin his career as a commoner from the very bottom without being able to take advantage of the progress made by his father. Thus, generation after generation an Islamic country witnessed the same process of building up fortunes from the smallest beginnings and undoing a life's work at death by the confiscation of the private property of the deceased man to the State and the reduction of his sons to the rank of poor commoners.

So much for the richer classes. As regards the common people, the Muslim State made no attempt to strengthen the nation, to develop the national character or to ensure the economic prosperity of the people. No independence of thought was allowed, and the grossest kind of flattery was expected and encouraged by the Court. Hence, no first-rate genius in literature or art was produced among the Indian Muhammadans.

The Court was the only centre of culture and the only nursery of the fine arts (if we except a few temples in the far-off South.) But the nation in general did not benefit by it and Court patronage had a really demoralising effect on creative genius. Hence, Hindu, and Muhammadan literature and art in mediaeval India fall far short of the productions of democratic Greece or England.

§9. Natural growth of the Hindus stopped.

Muslim rule also arrested the growth of the Hindus. At the first stage of the conquest, all our monasteries and rich temples were sacked and thus the centres of Hindu learning were destroyed. No powerful Hindu Rajah was left to serve as a patron of Sanskrit scholars and authors. In consequence, Sanskrit learning virtually died out of mediaeval India, what little was left of it, was extremely barren and consisted of logical subtleties, elaboration of rituals, new editions of Canon law, commentaries, and commentaries on commentaries. Thus, North India was intellectually a desert from 1200 to 1550 A.D. It was only under Akbar that with Tulsidas in Hindi and the Vaishnav writers in Bengali, a great Hindu literature reappeared but in the vernacular. The same Emperor founded a truly national Court and under him there was a great upheaval of the Indian intellect.

§10. Why did the Indian Muhammadans deteriorate?

A minute study of the history of Mughal India gives one a clear impression of the rapid decline of the Muslim aristocracy and gentry settled in India. The rapidity and sureness of this decline are partly concealed by the genius and character of many of the converts from Hinduism and fresh immigrants from Persia or Central Asia. But it is equally striking that the grandsons of the last two classes on the Indian soil became hopelessly degenerate.

The first cause of this phenomenon was a reckless crossbreeding and the maintenance of harems filled with women of all sorts of races castes and stages of civilisation. The children of such unions represented a much lower intellectual type than pure Hindus, pure Persians, or pure Turks.

Too much wealth, when accompanied by the peace and order which the Mughal empire gave to the land, fostered luxury among the Muhammadan upper classes and their position as the dominant race fostered pride and idleness. Hereditary aristorcracies have a natural tendency to deteriorate and the process is checked only by hard work in the army or civil administration and other kinds of healthy activity such as participation in the free public life of a democratic country or a spirit of adventure and exploration. But these correctives were wanting among the sons of the Mughal peers, to whom the emperors always left a portion of their fathers earnings and gave fairly high posts by reason of their birth.

The Indian Muhammadans could not retain Persian or Turkish as their mother-tongue and yet they did not cultivate any Indian vernacular for literary purposes. They were ashamed to write in the zaban-i-Hindavi (i.e., Hindustani) which they spoke in the home, the office, the street, and the camp. The desperate and ruinous attempt to cling to Persian as the language of official correspondence, serious and elegant literature, and polished society, while Hindustani was their mother-tongue, was continued by the Indian Muhammadans till about 1750, when Hindustani was frankly accepted as their literary language. This linguistic difficulty accounts for the literary barrenness of the Indian Muhammadans, and it greatly retarded the spread of real education during the Mughal period.

The Muhammadans of India, particularly those of Turkish and Afghan breeds, are a military race but not eminently intellectual nor industrial. Hence, they began to decline when the utmost possible limit of their conquest was reached.

The degradation of women in the harems of the rich naturally tends to degrade their children. The evil took a more aggravated form in India than in Arabia or Persia, where few could afford to support more wives than one and these wives were of the same race as their husbands.

§11. Failure of Mughal empire due to lacli of the spirit of progress and self-correction.

The student of mediaeval Indian history cannot fail to be struck by the fact that the Mughal empire became a hopeless failure in the 18th century, though it had splendid resources behind it and had achieved much for India in the 16 th and 17th centuries. In the 18th century, Mughal civilisation was like a spent bullet and the downfall of the Mughal empire was only a question of time, even if no Nadir Shah or Ahmad Abdali had appeared in India.

The first and foremost cause of this phenomenon is the contrast between the spirit of all oriental monarchies and that of a modern civilised empire like the British. Such a modern empire contains an element of self-criticism and reform within itself. Hence, any new defect or source of decay in it is promptly detected and remedied before it can become incurable. Not so oriental monarchies or even European monarchies of the ancient world, like the Roman and Macedonian.

Secondly, oriental monarchies are essentially dependent upon the personality of the sovereign and in some cases also on the character of the ruling minority. The British empire, on the other hand, is democratic; it is the domination of much of the world by the entire British race and other races absorbed into the British, —and not by an individual king or family. Hence, though the ruling British families of one generation may degenerate in the next, streams of fresh and able rulers of men rise from the ranks of the British race to take their places. In Mughal India, on the other hand, the degeneration of the India-born Muhammadans was rapid and striking, and nothing could remedy it, as there was no popular education, no public discussion, no social reform. The supply of able adventurers from beyond the Khaibar pass who had contributed to the glories of the reigns of Akbar and Shah Jahan ceased and the decay in the ruling families of India could not be arrested by the infusion of new blood either from among the mass of the local people or from among foreign immigrants.

It was the fatal defect of Mughal rule that it always continued to bear the character of a military occupation of the land and did not try to build up a nation or a homogeneous state. The glories of Agra and Delhi in the golden days of Shah Jahan ought not to blind us to the fact that the Mughal Emperors never followed the first principle of political science, viz., that "There cannot be a great empire without a great people."

Under even the best of them, though there were great ministers and generals, the mass of the people remained "Human Sheep" as in the worst days of the past. The Englishmen who defeated the Indian Nawabs and Maharajahs may have been a handful of men—some of them not even professional soldiers; but they had behind them the enormous reservoir of the British democracy with all its collective talents and resources, while our Nawabs and Maharajahs had behind them none but a few self-seeking followers and hireling troops. They did not lead any national opposition to the foreign conquerors.

Islam, as interpreted after the failure of the rationalistic (mutazala) movement in the Court of the early Abbaside Khalifs of Baghdad, became too rigid, too inelastic and incapable of adapting itself to changes of environment. It has all the strength and weakness of a strictly dogmatic creed like Calvinism. The rigidity of Islam has enabled its followers in all lands to succeed up to a certain point. But there they have stopped, while progress is the rule of the living world. At the same time that Europe has been steadily advancing, the stationary Muhammadans have been relatively falling back and every year has increased the distance between Europe and Asia in knowledge, organisation, accumulated resources and acquired capacity and made it increasingly difficult for the Asiatics to compete with the Europeans. The English conquest of the Mughal empire is only a part of the inevitable domination of all Africa and Asia by the European nations, —which is only another way of saying that the progressive races are replacing the conservative ones, just as enterprising families replace sleepy indolent ones in the leadership of our own society. Therefore, if we wish to profit by the study of our country's history.

------- *Forward, forward let us range.*

Let the great world spin for ever down the ringing grooves of change.

LIST OF TITLES WITH ISBN NO.

ISBN	TITLE
9788194914129	1984
9789390575220	1984 & Animal Farm (2In1)
9789390575572	1984 & Animal Farm (2In1): The International Best-Selling Classics
9789390575848	35 Sonnets
9789390575329	A Clergyman's Daughter
9789390575923	A Study In Scarlet
9789390896097	A Tale Of Two Cities
9789390896837	Abide in Christ
9789390896202	Abraham Lincoln
9789390896912	Absolute Surrender
9789390896608	African American Classic Collection
9789390575305	Aldous Huxley: The Collected Works
9789390896141	An Autobiography of M. K. Gandhi
9789390575886	Animal Farm
9789390575619	Animal Farm & The Great Gatsby (2In1)
9789390575626	Animal Farm & We
9789390896158	Anna Karenina
9789390575534	Antic Hay
9789390896165	Antony & Cleopatra
9789390896172	As I Lay Dying
9789390896226	As You like it
9789390575671	At Your Command
9789390575350	Awakened Imagination
9789390575114	Be What You Wish
9789390896233	Believe In yourself
9789390896998	Best of Charles Darwin: The Origin of Species & Autobiography
9789390896684	Best Of Horror : Dracula And Frankenstein
9789390575503	Best Of Mark Twain (The Adventures of Tom Sawyer AND The Adventures of Huckleberry Finn)
9789390896769	Black History Collection
9789390575756	Brave New World, Animal Farm & 1984 (3in1)

9789390896240	Brother Karamzov
9789390575053	Bulleh Shah Poetry
9789390575725	Burmese Days
9789390896257	Bushido
9789390896066	Can't Hurt Me
9788194914112	Chanakya Neeti: With The Complete Sutras
9789390896042	Crime and Punishment
9789390575527	Crome Yellow
9789390575046	Down and Out in Paris and London
9789390896844	Dracula
9789390575442	Emersons Essays: The Complete First & Second Series (Self-Reliance & Other Essays)
9789390575749	Emma
9789390575817	Essential Tozer Collection - The Pursuit of God & The Purpose of Man
9789390896578	Fascism What It Is and How to Fight It
9789390575688	Feeling is the Secret
9789390575190	Five Lessons
9789390575954	Frankenstein
9789390575237	Franz Kafka: Collected Works
9789390575282	Franz Kafka: Short Stories
9789390575060	George Orwell Collected Works
9789390575077	George Orwell Essays
9789390575213	George Orwell Poems
9788194914150	Greatest Poetry Ever Written Vol 1
9788194914143	Greatest Poetry Ever Written Vol 1
9789390896301	Gulliver's Travel
9789390575961	Gunaho Ka Devta
9789390575893	H. P. Lovecraft Selected Stories Vol 1
9789390575978	H. P. Lovecraft Selected Stories Vol 2
9789390896059	Hamlet
9789390575022	His Last Bow: Some Reminiscences of Sherlock Holmes
9789390896134	History of Western Philosophy
9789390575121	Homage To Catalonia

9789390896219	How to develop self-confidence and Improve public Speaking
9789390896295	How to enjoy your life and your Job
9789390575633	How to own your own mind
9789390896318	How to read Human Nature
9789390896325	How to sell your way through the life
9789390896370	How to use the laws of mind
9789390896387	How to use the power of prayer
9789390896028	How to win friends & Influence People
9788194824176	How To Win Friends and Influence People
9789390896103	Humility The Beauty of Holiness
9789390896653	Imperialism the Highest Stage of Capitalism
9789390575084	In Our Time
9789390575169	In Our Time & Three Stories and Ten poems
9789390575145	James Allen: The Collected Works
9789390896189	Jesus Himself
9789390575480	Jo's Boys
9789390896394	Julius Caesar
9789390575404	Keep the Aspidistra Flying
9789390896400	Kidnapped
9789390896424	King Lear
9789390575824	Lady Susan
9789390896455	Law of Success
9789390896264	Lincoln The Unknown
9789390575565	Little Men
9789390575640	Little Women
9788194914174	Lost Horizon
9789390896462	Macbeth
9789390896929	Man Eaters of Kumaon
9789390896523	Man The Dwelling Place of God
9789390896349	Man The Dwelling Place of God
9789390575909	Mansfield Park
9788194914136	Manto Ki 25 Sarvshreshth Kahaniya
9789390896509	Marxism, Anarchism, Communism
9789390575664	Mathematical Principles of Natural Philosophy

9788194914198	Meditations
9789390575800	Mein Kampf
9789390575794	Memory How To Develop, Train, And Use It
9789390896486	Mind Power
9789390896585	Money
9789390575039	Mortal Coils
9789390575770	My Life and Work
9789390896035	Narrative of the Life of Frederick Douglass
9789390575152	Neville Goddard: The Collected Works
9789390575985	Northanger Abbey
9789390896530	Notes From Underground
9789390896547	Oliver Twist
9789390575459	On War
9789390575541	One, None and a Hundred Thousand
9789390896554	Othelo
9789390575435	Out Of This World
9789390575015	Persuasion
9789390575510	Prayer The Art Of Believing
9789390575091	Pride and Prejudice
9789390896561	Psychic Perception
9789390575381	Rabindranath Tagore - 5 Best Short Stories Vol 2
9789390575367	Rabindranath Tagore - Short Stories (Masters Collections Including The Childs Return)
9789390575374	Rabindranath Tagore 5 Best Short Stories Vol 1 (Including The Childs Return
9789390896622	Romeo & Juliet
9789390896127	Sanatana Dharma
9789390575596	Seedtime & Harvest
9789390896639	Selected Stories of Guy De Maupassant
9789390575206	Self-Reliance & Other Essays
9789390575176	Sense and Sensibility
9789390575299	Shyamchi Aai
9789390896738	Socialism Utopian and Scientific
9789390896646	Success Through a Positive Mental Attitude
9789390575428	The Adventures of Huckleberry Finn

9789390575183	The Adventures of Sherlock Holmes
9789390575343	The Adventures of Tom Sawyer
9789390896691	The Alchemy Of Happiness
9789390575862	The Art Of Public Speaking
9789390896288	The Autobiography Of Charles Darwin
9788194914181	The Best of Franz Kafka: The Metamorphosis & The Trial
9789390575008	The Call Of Cthulhu and Other Weird Tales
9789390575107	The Case-Book of Sherlock Holmes
9789390896110	The Castle Of Otranto
9789390896745	The Communist Manifesto
9789390575589	The Complete Fiction of H. P. Lovecraft
9789390575497	The Complete Works of Florence Scovel Shinn
9789390896820	The Conquest of Breard
9789390896813	The Diary of a Young Girl
9789390896332	The Diary of a Young Girl The Definitive Edition of the Worlds Most Famous Diary
9789390575701	The Great Gatsby, Animal Farm & 1984 (3In1)
9789390575312	The Greatest Works Of George Orwell (5 Books) Including 1984 & Non-Fiction
9789390575992	The Hound of Baskervilles
9789390896707	The Idiot
9789390896714	The Invisible Man
9789390575657	The Knowledge of the holy
9789390575558	The Law & the Promise
9789390896721	The Law Of Attraction
9789390896776	The Leader in you
9789390896363	The Life of Christ
9789390896196	The Man-Eating Leopard of Rudraprayag
9789390896783	The Master Key to Riches
9789390575268	The Memoirs Of Sherlock Holmes
9789390896479	The Midsummer Night's Dream
9789390575466	The Mill On The Floss
9789390896790	The Miracles of your mind
9789390896660	The Mutual Aid A Factor in Evolution
9789390896448	The Origin of Species

9789390896905	The Peter Kropotkin Anthology The Conquest of Bread & Mutual Aid A Factor of Evolution
9789390896806	The Picture of Dorian Gray
9789390896271	The Picture of Dorian Gray
9789390575275	The Power Of Awareness
9789390896356	The Power of Concentration
9788194824169	The Power of Positive Thinking
9789390575411	The Power of the Spoken Word
9788194914105	The Power Of Your Subconscious Mind
9789390896899	The Power of Your Subconscious Mind
9789390896417	The Principles of Communism
9789390575787	The Psychology Of Mans Possible Evolution
9789390896615	The Psychology of Salesmanship
9789390575732	The Pursuit of God
9789390575398	The Pursuit of Happiness
9789390896851	The Quick and Easy Way to effective Speaking
9789390575947	The Return Of Sherlock Holmes
9789390575138	The Road To Wigan Pier
9789390896981	The Root of the Righteous
9789390575855	The Science Of Being Well
9788194914167	The Science Of Getting Rich, The Science Of Being Great & The Science Of Being Well (3In1)
9789390896011	The Screwtape Letters
9789390896073	The Screwtape Letters
9789390575336	The Secret Door to Success
9789390575695	The Secret Of Imagining
9789390896868	The Secret Of Success
9789390896431	The Seven Last Words
9789390575930	The Sign of the Four
9789390896004	The Sonnets
9789390896516	The Souls of Black Folk
9789390896875	The Sound and The Fury
9789390575244	The State and Revolution
9789390896882	The Story of My Life
9789390896936	The Story Of Oriental Philosophy

9789390896752	The Strange Case of Dr. Jekyll and Mr. Hyde
9789390896943	The Tempest
9789390575916	The Valley Of Fear
9789390575879	The Wind in the willows
9789390896080	The Wind in the willows
9789390575763	Their eyes were watching gofd
9789390575831	Three Stories
9789390896950	Twelfth Night
9789390896592	Twelve Years a Slave
9789390896677	Up from Slavery
9789390896974	Value Price and Profit
9789390896967	Wake Up and Live
9789390896493	With Christ in the School of Prayer
9789390575602	Your Faith is Your Fortune
9789390575473	Your Infinite Power To Be Rich
9789390575251	Your Word is Your Wand
9789390575718	Youth
9789391316099	A Christmas Carol
9789391316105	A Doll's House
9789391316501	A Passage to India
9789391316709	A Portrait of the Artist as a Young Man
9789391316112	A Tale of Two Cities
9789391316747	A Tear and a Smile
9789391316167	Agnes Gray
9789391316174	Alice's Adventures in Wonderland
9789391316136	Anandamath
9789391316181	Anne Of Green Gables
9789391316754	Anthem
9789391316198	Around The World in 80 Days
9789391316013	As A Man Thinketh
9789391316242	Autobiography of a Yogi
9789391316266	Beyond Good and Evil
9789391316761	Bleak House
9789391316778	Chitra, a Play in One Act
9789391316310	David Copperfield

9789391316075	Demian
9789391316785	Dubliners
9789391316051	Favourite Tales from the Arabian Nights
9789391316235	Gitanjali
9789391316068	Gravity
9789391316150	Great Speeches of Abraham Lincoln
9789391316662	Guerilla Warfare
9789391316839	Kim
9789391316822	Mother
9789391316211	My Childhood
9789391316846	Nationalism
9789391316327	Oliver Twist
9789391316853	Pygmalion
9789391316334	Relativity: The Special and the General Theory
9789391316389	Scientific Healing Affirmation
9789391316341	Sons and Lovers
9789391316587	Tales from India
9789391316372	Tess of The D'Urbervilles
9789391316396	The Awakening and Selected Stories
9789391316402	The Bhagvad Gita
9789391316303	The Book of Enoch
9789391316228	The Canterville Ghost
9789391316907	The Dynamic Laws of Prosperity
9789391316006	The Great Gatsby
9789391316860	The Hungry Stones and Other Stories
9789391316433	The Idiot
9789391316440	The Importance of Being Earnest
9789391316297	The Light of Asia
9789391316914	The Madman His Parables and Poems
9789391316457	The Odyssey
9789391316921	The Picture of Dorian Gray
9789391316464	The Prince
9789391316938	The Prophet
9789391316945	The Republic
9789391316518	The Scarlet Letter

9789391316143	The Seven Laws of Teaching
9789391316525	The Story of My Experiments with Truth
9789391316532	The Tales of the Mother Goose
9789391316549	The Thirty Nine Steps
9789391316594	The Time Machine
9789391316600	The Turn of the Screw
9789391316983	The Upanishads
9789391316617	The Yellow Wallpaper
9789391316426	The Yoga Sutras of Patanjali
9789391316990	Ulysses
9789391316624	Utopia
9789391316679	Vanity Fair
9789391316020	What Is To Be Done
9789391316686	Within A Budding Grove
9789391316693	Women in Love